MW01114197

GILGAL

BIBLICAL PRINCIPLES GOVERNING TRANSITION
INTO THE APOSTOLIC REFORMATION

THAMO NAIDOO

Copyright © 2016– by Thamo Naidoo

Publisher—eGenCo

All rights reserved. This book is protected by the copyright laws of the United States of America. This book may not be copied or reprinted for commercial gain or profit. The use of short quotations or occasional page copying for personal or group study is permitted and encouraged. Permission for other usages must be obtained from eGenCo or the author.
Unless otherwise indicated, Scripture quotations are taken from the New King James Version®. Copyright © 1982 by Thomas Nelson, Inc. Used by permission. All rights reserved. Scripture quotations marked KJV are taken from the King James Version of the Bible. Public domain. Originally Printed in the Republic of South Africa. © 2004 by Thamo Naidoo

Generation Culture Transformation
Specializing in publishing for generation culture change

eGenCo
824 Tallow Hill Road
Chambersburg, PA 17202, USA
Phone: 717-461-3436
Email: info@egen.co
Website: www.egen.co

facebook.com/egenbooks   pinterest.com/eGenDMP
youtube.com/egenpub   twitter.com/eGenDMP
egen.co/blog   instagram.com/egenco_dmp

Publisher's Cataloging-in-Publication Data
Naidoo, Thamo.
Gilgal.; by Thamo Naidoo.
152 pages cm.
ISBN: 978-1-68019-999-4 paperback
        978-1-68019-800.3 ebook
        978-1-68019-801-1 ebook
1. Religion. 2. Apostolic Reformation. 3. Reconfiguration. I. Title
2016903270

Dedication

This book is dedicated to the memory of the late Aaron Govender, who was suddenly called to rest on the 3rd of September 2004, the month of the first publication of this book. He was not just an integral part of the Eldership of *River of Life Christian Ministries*, but also a colleague and friend. In many respects he was a source of inspiration and motivation to me in writing *Gilgal*. His mark on my life has left an imprint on every page of this book.

Table of Contents

Foreword

We are living in the most powerful prophetic time in the destiny of the nations. The release of strong apostolic impartation into the foundation of Church life is activating the saints into recapturing their global mandate and establishing God's will and Kingdom upon the entire earth. God's most profound desire is to establish a standard nation in the earth, one to which all other nations can conform.

The Father has foreordained that His prophetic register, out from which His purposes will find culmination in the earth, will converge in a representative people who will know how to bring the nations of the earth to a position of "bended knee." God's intent is for the Church to occupy a position of patriarchal strength in the earth. It's a position from which His Fatherhood identity is imposed so that the Church can birth forth His purpose in every generation.

Patriarchal strength means that the Church cannot be static. It is the catalyst that propels God's authority to be executed in the earth. The end-time Church is an authoritative vehicle that engineers a shift in spiritual positions. It is this powerful position in God that excludes "worldly indulgence."

The last-day Church will be a mountain, a fortress, a tower (Isa. 2) positioned in the midst of the crises that will overtake the earth! In Daniel's vision, the stone of the Kingdom was cut out of a mountain (Dan. 2:45) and it began to destroy the Babylonian systems of the earth. The stone itself grew and became a mountain in the earth.

In the context of this book, *Gilgal: Biblical Principles Governing Transition Into the Apostolic Reformation* is powerfully relevant in that it imparts the present truth realities of the transition of the entire Church into governmental superiority. Thamo encapsulates accurately a key ingredient to the 21st century Kingdom dominion.

Gilgal…this word means more than just *"rolling away the reproach"* of a past life; it symbolically portrays the picture of the birth of a nation! It gives us a vivid picture of the emergence of a new breed of people—healed from every fragmentation within the Body of Christ; people with fresh insight and powerfully positioned for final conquest!

At Gilgal, a whole nation was built through the process of circumcision—*the cutting away of excess flesh from the frontlets of their mentalities.* Thamo accurately exegetes the practical principles of this process that are God's prerequisites for stepping into a place of final conquest. Thamo Naidoo has travelled the nations teaching these new present truth positions of the Lord. It is my fervent prayer that pastors and Church leaders begin to teach these principles in their local churches so that the message of the Apostolic Reformation can be embraced and, consequently, position the Church into new levels in God.

Shaun Blignaut
Father's Heart Ministries
Port Elizabeth, South Africa

Preface

The seed that gave birth to this book can be traced to 1998. I was in prayer in a hotel room in Nakuru, Kenya, when the Holy Spirit illuminated my heart with the revelation of Gilgal. I heard God say to me that I must write a book on Gilgal, a book which will help congregations to transition into the new season. In a moment, I received the outline that is now the framework of this present copy.

At that point in time, the message of the Apostolic Reformation was fairly new to me. It had dynamically impacted my life, but I was not ready to deliver the message. Although I was overwhelmed by the instruction to write the book, I was also intimidated by the mere thought of writing (a skill I lacked). As a result of my feelings of inability, unbelief, intimidation and poor discipline, the book has taken six years to complete. Needless to say, writing this book has been one of the most daunting challenges of my life. It was like a first attempt at climbing a high mountain.

I must, however, acknowledge those who motivated me to bring conclusion to this outstanding matter on my prophetic register. My wife, Mirolyn, has not only encouraged the completion of the book but also made invaluable suggestions in its formation. My sons Theron, Sherwin and Rylan have also made many sacrifices in permitting me to travel the nations and to give me the space to hide in my office for hours so that the writing could be completed.

My special thanks to Dr. Rani Moodley and Pastor Winston Govinden for their insightful suggestions, and to Kenny Frank for editing. My sincere gratitude to Living Word Church (Ps. Eugene and Patrice Sheppard), Washington DC and Crusaders West (Apostle Daryl O Neil), Chicago, USA, for their financial support and encouragement in the writing of this book. There are so many others who have played a role in giving momentum to its writing; Leon and Hendrika Brown (Alaska, USA) and Eric and Carolyn Warren (Columbus, Ohio, USA).

I would like to place on record my appreciation to Dr. Noel Woodroffe of the World Breakthrough Network for the impact made on my life in the formative stages of the apostolic season. He together with Dr Robert Munien, helped shape this message in my life and ministry.

Finally, my congregation and staff of **River of Life Christian Ministries** occupy a very unique place in this book. Apart from the fact that their support has been a catalyst in spurring me to finish the book, they are also the *model* that has tested and proven the principles gleaned from Gilgal. Yet it is with sadness that the first publication of this book is released in the same month that my colleague Aaron Govender suddenly died. He was not only a fellow elder in our congregation but also a wise counsellor and a high-ranking general in the Kingdom of God. His mark on my life has left an imprint on every page of this book. This book is dedicated to his memory.

Thamo Naidoo

Introduction

The winds of change are blowing over the Church and the global community. A new season has dawned upon humanity, creating conditions for the Holy Spirit to introduce new biblical strategies, designs and mandates for expediting the divine purpose in the earth. The Scriptures concur:

> *To everything there is a season, a time for every purpose*
> *under heaven* (Ecclesiastes 3:1).

The new discloses the predestined designs for the fulfilment of God's sovereign will in the earth. Therefore, it is crucial for Church leaders to adjust their structures, visions, leadership styles and all other operations to the principal mission of that season. This implies that everything in the Church has to go through the process of revision and re-evaluation. Essentially, the Church is the microcosm of everything that is in the heart of God. Hence, it must be the most accurate reflection of the divine desire in the earth.

Change carries the spirit of reformation that confronts every sphere and system of governance in the earth. When the seasons change, everything in human history is affected. Consequently, everything must go through the radical evolutionary process of transition. The primary goal of any divinely initiated season is to aggressively advance the Kingdom of God towards its predestined conclusion. It is in this regard that it is incumbent upon the Church to become the embodiment of the mind of God in the earth by modelling, through tangible structures, everything that is locked up in the heart of God. The Church is the mechanism through which the wisdom of God is manifest to the principalities and powers in all of creation. In this fact lies the apostolicity of the Church—that is, her ability to act accurately as the agency of God in the earth.

Leaders of congregations should make every attempt to both seek and to know the mind and counsel of God for the season. It is also envisaged that leaders will prepare their congregations to make the necessary adjustments. This involves the process of restructuring the mindsets of the people and modifying any physical structures that sustain religious life in their congregations. From this emerges the challenging responsibility of altering (or modifying) the composition of those "sacred" systems that strictly maintain religious activity but do not produce spiritual life or the desired objectives of the new season. If there is insensitivity to the expectations of a new season, there is also the danger of religiously guarding a system of thought and a structure of practice that are no longer relevant to the purposes of God. Often, there is the emergence of a concerted attempt to jealously guard and preserve a past heritage. The consequence is an abandonment of the desire to be relevant to the present process. Instead of advocating God's purpose in the earth, there is the peril of becoming an adversary of the divine intent. Those who adopt this position can easily become programme-orientated and activity-driven, although they are not directed by the purposes of God.

The Christian faith is a journey that presents a heavenly way of life. Therefore, believers in the early Church were aptly referred to as the people of the Way.[1] The journey of the believer is intrinsically spiritual but lived out in the natural. In this respect, the spiritual aspect of the journey must superimpose and radically influence the natural course of an individual's existence. Essentially the history (Greek *chronos*[2]) of humanity must be governed by the seasons (Greek *kairos*[3]) of God. When a new season (*kairos*) of God is clearly revealed to His people, places are named as a memorial of that significant "time" in the history of humanity. This point is clearly reflected in the life and experience of the pilgrimage of the patriarchs. Whenever they had a specific encounter with their God, the milieu of that unique encounter was named or renamed. In a sense, these places highlight a significant milestone in salvation history. Although these places were unique moments in redemptive history, they do relay to us, the Church of Jesus Christ, examples that can be guiding lights in our journey to the Promised Land, or to the Lord Himself.

Presently, there are many Church leaders who are recognizing the need to change the existing structure of their congregations.

---

[1] Acts 9:2; 19:9, 23; 22:4; 24:14, 22.

[2] *Chronos* is the scientific measure of time. It refers to "time quantitatively as a period measured by a succession of objects and events and denotes the passing of moments." "It has only length, not challenge of accomplishment, as *kairos*" (S. Zodiates, ref. 5550, p. 1769).

[3] *Kairos* in its literal meaning refers to "season, opportune time, fixed time" (S. Zodiates, ref. 2540, p. 1726). Metaphorically it is the spiritual measure of a set time that is determined by the human response to the divine task at hand. It is the time that provides one with opportunities to collaborate with destiny in fulfilling the purposes of God in the earth.

Some do not know *how* and *what* to do to effect the process of transition. Others have, in their zeal, impulsively (and probably unwisely) introduced changes that have received resistance, indifference and a migration of people from their congregations. This results in frustration and disillusionment with the idea of change. However, there are some leaders who are ignorant of the fact that when a season changes they are required to make adjustments accordingly. It is ignorance or insensitivity to the unfolding plans of God that keep their congregations in the wilderness of barrenness and in the practice of mundane religious activity.

There is also that category of Church leaders who are fearful of changing their structures, strategies and programs. They believe that by introducing change to their existing way of religious life, they may contravene the divine will, consequently falling into error. They are of the opinion that if God gave them these patterns in the past, then these cannot be changed. However, this may not necessarily be a correct assumption. A study of the pattern for building the tabernacle provides an example of the dynamic process of development that reached its consummate manifestation in Jesus Christ. In this regard, it can be deduced that while the physical shape of the tabernacle was continually going through the process of change, the core values and principles of God that directed the building of the tabernacle did not change. For example, the process that led to the tabernacle being built by Moses had become obsolete when Solomon built the temple. Yet the building of the Temple of Solomon did not contradict the Tabernacle of Moses. While the Temple of Solomon fully embraced the pattern of Moses' Tabernacle, it went further by amplifying, clarifying and defining the divine intent for the construction of the tabernacle in the first place. Each phase in the development of the tabernacle was an upgrade that highlighted the intent of God in the establishment and continuity of His purpose in the earth.

It is with this in mind that I have written this book. The primary objective of the book is to share principles that will assist those leaders who are desirous of taking their congregations through the painful process of transition. These principles have been gleaned from my personal experiences as I embarked on the journey of discovering His will for the congregation I shepherd. However, in writing this book, I have consciously restrained myself from using personal examples from my own journey of transition, since they may shade the application of the principles of change in the unique places at which Church leaders may find their congregations.

Biblical principles in this book can guide Church leaders in the implementation of change within their congregations. At the same time, I must emphatically point out that these are not necessarily all the principles involved in the dynamic process of transition. I am aware of the fact that there may be many more invaluable principles and lessons that one can use to navigate and guide one into God's will for His Church.

I also write from the presupposition that while the Bible is replete with examples of external structures (built by people) undergoing the process of metamorphosis, the divine principles in Scripture are immutable—*these never change*. Although the divine methods are continuously changing, the divine principle(s) are never contradicted. Whenever the seasons change, the principles from the previous season(s) are exported, installed and adapted to the new season. Furthermore, new revelations (from the Word of God) are introduced by the new season, adding new principles to the evolutionary process of growth in unfolding divine mystery. This point is highlighted in Hebrews:

> *See that you do not refuse Him who speaks. For if they*
> *did not escape who refused Him who spoke on earth,*
> *much more shall we not escape if we turn away from*
> *Him who speaks from heaven, whose voice then shook*
> *the earth; but now He has promised, saying, "Yet once*
> *more I shake not only the earth, but also heaven."*
> *Now this, "Yet once more," indicates the **removal** [my*
> emphasis] *of those things that are being shaken, as of*
> *things that are made, that the things which cannot be*
> *shaken may remain* (Hebrews 12:25-27).

Implied in the word "removal" (Greek *metathesis*) is the process of God critically evaluating everything that is "made" by human agency in the Church. The intention is that, that which has passed the divine test may remain as an integral part of the evolution of His purposes in the earth. This infers that only that which is of a more excellent heavenly quality should be a constituent part of the construct of what God is building. In the light of this, it can be asserted that there is a continuous divine process of elimination that must take place in the Church. Ultimately, only the substance of things that are eternal in their nature will remain.

It is so amazing to note that the revelation of a divine pattern is always true to the foundational principles. To put it plainly, *the statutes and precepts of God never change, but God's methods of establishing His purpose in humanity are constantly evolving.* "It is simply marvellous how God has kept everything true to principle: one never finds later, however fully a thing is developed, that there is a change in principle; the principle is there and one cannot get away from it."[4]

---

[4] Sparks, *Prophetic Ministry,*p. 2.

Although there are multifarious ways in which God reveals His plans and purposes to His people, there is, however, no contradiction to His character and nature or to His revealed plans for His people. The writer of Hebrews assertively makes this point in his opening statements:

> *God, who at various times and in various ways spoke in time past to the fathers by the prophets* (Hebrews 1:1).

From this verse, we glean that God has been in continuous communication with humanity. He did this *"at various times"* (Greek *polumeros*) or at different times and stages in human history. He also revealed His will *"in various ways"* (Greek *polutropos*) or in different manners compatible with their ability to comprehend. In other words, He used the most contemporary ways or methodologies to communicate with people. Throughout the Old Testament, it is abundantly clear that God related to the people on the level of their comprehension. The Prophets were not just used as passive instruments of communication but He indwelled their lives and through them demonstrated His will to the people. Everything they communicated or built was true to the divine principles and without a contradiction of the Scriptures—although they communicated in different epochs and by utilising different methods.

On this point, it can be argued that no matter what God communicates or builds in the earth, these are always true to the divine principles. "We may take as settled that if in the superstructure there is anything that is out of harmony with God's original basic spiritual principle that is going to be a defect which will spell tragedy sooner or later. The superstructure, in every detail of principle, has to be true to the foundation, to the original."[5] Therefore, we can agree that the Church is God's superstructure in the earth. Its very nature and operation is governed by the divine principles that do not contradict the Scriptures. Basically, it can be stated that the fundamental principles of God are transferred from an old season into a new season, although the structure that originally housed these principles may have been dismantled.

Moreover, in every new season, new principles are unravelled, thereby giving momentum and greater definition to the formative process of building, into earthly structures, the purposes of God. These structures should be "more accurate" than those structures that reflected "accurately" (at a previous point in time) the revelation of that unique season.

We must, at all times, bear in mind that the Church is on a journey of progressively developing into the exact representation and image of Christ in the earth. Each season restores an integral part of Christ that contributes to the Church's construction in the earth. Like the Prophets, who communicated the will of God to the people, Church leaders must create the environment and conditions for God to speak in and through them. These leaders must develop an operational system in their congregations that capture the essential messages of any given season. They must allow the purpose of that season to shape, form and express the revelation of God. Whatever they receive as a revelation must be validated and confirmed by the Scriptures—that is, by a *"more sure word of prophecy."*[6] Accessing the present truth from God will not contradict the Scriptures. The Word of God is the plumb line

---

[5] Iibid.

[6] 2 Peter 1:19 KJV.

that establishes every revelation undergirding the legitimacy of a new season in the earth.

It is anticipated that *Gilgal* will contribute to this revelation by proposing to Church leaders the principles that will help the process of transition. In this way, checks and balances can be put in place for the development of healthy New Testament apostolic congregations.

CHAPTER 1

Apostolic Reformation

A new season has dawned upon the Church of Jesus Christ, labelled in some circles as the Apostolic Reformation.[7] It comes in the form of a clarion call from the throne of God for a consummate reformation of gigantic proportions to be imposed upon the Church. Arguably, this title aptly captures the mind of God and describes the fundamental features that characterise this epoch in redemptive history.

Accompanying the purpose of God for the season is the restoration of the office and ministry of Prophets and Apostles to the fivefold ministry of the government of the Church. These ministry gifts feature prominently in the whole mission of God for this season. They play a significant role in articulating the divine intent and also providing the grace gifts for the Church to finish the assignment of the season. Some of the ensuing chapters will attempt to examine their role in this season.

---

[7] Dr. Noel Woodroffe of the World Breakthrough Network arguably has been recognized as the author of this title.

Apostolic Reformation Defined

The word "apostolic" derived from the Greek verb *apostello* literally means, "to send off, out, forth."[8] It denotes a specific "sending" (on a specific mission) by the "sender" (God) that imposes a clear mandate on the "sent one" (the Church). Included in this "sending" is the idea of an intimate relationship between the "sender" and the "sent one" and that the "sent one" adopts a voluntary and a subservient attitude to the sender. It indicates strict adherence to the specific details of the mission without deviating from the prescribed instructions. In the context of this book, it refers to the exact nature and detail of the *missio dei* (mission of God) for His Church.

The word "reformation" (Greek *diorthosis*[9]) defines the nature and content of the Apostolic Reformation. From a literal standpoint, it means to "make straight either by a right arrangement and right ordering or by making an amendment and bringing right again."[10] It conveys the idea of setting in order again that which has been made imperfect or marred by sin in the Church and in Creation. The imposition of reformation comes at a time when the imperfect or the inadequate must be superseded by a "better" (more accurate) order of things.

The spirit of this Reformation calls for a forensic inquiry into the existing structure and content of the Church and the definition of her ministry in the earth. The inquiry is not merely diagnostic in its approach, but it presents a *prognosis* of the problems highlighted. In a sense, it is similar to the ministry of Jeremiah.[11]

---

[8] S. Zodhiates, ref. 649, p. 1810.

[9] Hebrews 9:10.

[10] S. Zodhiates, ref. 1357, p. 1708.

[11] Jeremiah 1:10.

It does not merely *"root out and pull down"* or *"destroy and throw down,"* but it seeks to *"build and plant."* It understands that there cannot be *analysis* without *synthesis*. Hence, it presents to the Church constructive biblical patterns for building correctly. The underlying motivation is not a cosmetic or superficial rearrangement of the furniture of the Church, but a transformation of every inaccurate position of the Church. In essence, the message postulates that there must be a changing of *"wineskins"* before the *"new wine"* can be received.[12] Basically, it calls for a reformation of the structure and content of the Church before the Church can expect revival, renewal and the consummation of the end-time purposes of God.

The Scriptures model the conditions that activate reformation and describe the fundamental nature of the spirit of reformation. The ministry of Jesus Christ, the Lord of the Church, brought the greatest reformation to the earth that transformed the course of history and set the pattern and process for the restoration of *"all things."*[13] It is from this reformation that the standard and plumb line for all reformations are set. If there is to be any reformation in the earth, the lessons must be learned from His example. Christ is the dimension for whatever is done or accomplished in the earth. A study of Hebrews[14] will highlight some of the factors that govern the spirit of reformation.

The Biblical Factors Governing Reformation

The process of a reformation is activated by the divine conviction that change must be brought to the existing religious system

---

[12] Matthew 9:17.

[13] Acts 3:21.

[14] Hebrews 6–9.

in the Church. Consequently, whole systems of religious activity are made obsolete or brought back to the original order by the imposition of reformation.[15]

> *Concerned only with foods and drinks, various washings, and fleshly ordinances imposed until the **time of reformation** [emphasis mine]* (Hebrews 9:10).

The spirit of reformation arrives at that point in the Church when the system that sustains religious life has fully served its purpose and has become ineffective. As a result, reformation is the divine response at that decisive point when that which is *"growing old"* must immediately be terminated.[16] The "old" religious system is fading away or losing "heat" and therefore must give way to a new order of things. At that precise moment, reformation is activated and released. It is at that exact point when the old order or system has *fully* served its purpose or has become totally ineffective in contributing to the quality of the religious life of the Church. Hence, there is the need for the introduction of a new order of things. There cannot be a release of new things from the throne of God unless there is a change of existing structures. Only new wineskins can contain the new wine released by the Spirit of God.

> *Nor do they put new wine into old wineskins, or else the wineskins break, the wine is spilled, and the wineskins are ruined. But they put new wine into new wineskins, and both are preserved* (Matthew 9:17).

---

[15] Hebrews 9:10.

[16] Hebrews 8:13.

The Objective of Reformation

The spirit of reformation presents to the Church a *new and better way for drawing nearer to God.*[17] Whenever the spirit of reformation is released from the throne of God, its primary objective is to introduce the believer to a *"better"* order of things.[18] Reformation always brings with it the objective of upgrading religious systems so that believers can experience realms within the divine economy that are new to their worldview or have been shut off from them.

The purpose of reformation is driven by the desire to *"go on to perfection."*[19] It intends to take the Church beyond the foundational and elementary principles of religious activity.[20] The ultimate goal is to bring the believer to a *teleios* (a perfect, complete or matured) place in God. Maturity is the goal of the Christian life. The Church cannot function at the place of merely focussing on the elementary principles or foundational principles of the faith. Instead, the believer is encouraged to go beyond these principles. This does not mean a discarding of the foundational or elementary principles, but the utilisation of them, so that the lives of the believers can be configured and regulated in a way that manifests the fullness of Christ.

Reformation of Jesus Christ

Jesus Christ brought the greatest reformation to the earth. In Him is found the structure that determines the need for reformation in His Church. As the chief Apostle, He institutes the New

[17] Hebrews 10:20.
[18] Hebrews 8:6.
[19] Hebrews 6:1.
[20] Hebrews 6:1-12.

Covenant (new system of religion) that immediately concludes the Old Covenant (an old system of religion).[21]

A synoptic study of the two covenants clearly distinguishes and reveals the nature between the two covenants and thereby highlights the reasons why and when reformation is needed. By careful evaluation of the Old Covenant, one can extrapolate the original intention of God for the Church in the New Covenant. The Old Covenant was given to inform, mentor and instruct us (the Church) into the New Covenant. The old was a *type* of the new. It was given to guide the Church in her spiritual journey in God.

The Old Covenant (Old Testament)

Essentially the Old Covenant refers to a series of legally binding agreements that God had entered into with the fathers of Israel (over a long period of time) for the redemption of humanity. In these "agreements" is found the divine revelation and intent for the salvation of the human race and their reconciliation with the Creator. The Old Covenant expresses itself through a complex ceremonial system of religion that presents, to the Church of Jesus Christ, the pattern that ought to be carefully observed to enjoy a meaningful relationship with God.

A careful study of its very nature and complex day-to-day operation helps the believer to appreciate the work of salvation. Light is shed on the immense value of the shed blood of Jesus and the immediate benefit of direct access that one has to God without any elaborate ceremonial procedures. It is in this respect that an inquiry into the Old Covenant can help instruct us to understand the holy character of God and the need to avoid treating one's salvation indifferently or disrespectfully.

---

[21] Hebrews 3:1.

In essence, the entire Old Covenant revolved around an earthly sanctuary and religious services that placed undue restrictions on its devotees.[22] It just simply could not bring the devout to full spiritual satisfaction. The system was an external one reflecting outward religious activity. The reason for this, in my opinion, is that it would serve the New Testament Church with a *"copy and shadow of the heavenly things."*[23] The primary purpose of its existence was to reflect in a pictorial way the pattern and order of the heavenly structures. It also prophetically foreshadows the good things to come for the New Testament Church:

> *For the law, having a shadow of the good things to come, and not the very image of the things, can never with these same sacrifices, which they offer continually year by year, make those who approach perfect* (Hebrews 10:1).

It profiles how the heavenly sanctuary of God's eternal abode (New Testament Church) is to be structured. *"It was symbolic for the present time...."*[24] The ministry and structure of the sanctuary vividly communicated God's design for His timeless masterpiece—the Church of Jesus Christ. However, the "symbols" and "shadows" communicated through the ministry of the Old Covenant also highlighted the limitations of the system, since it was the model and not the actual. *"For if that first covenant had been faultless, then no place would have been sought for a second."*[25] It is

---

[22] Hebrews 9:1-9.

[23] Hebrews 8:5.

[24] Hebrews 9:9.

[25] Hebrews 8:7.

for this reason that the Scriptures enlighten us that its existence was for a certain period of time. It was not the eternal purpose of God, but a phase in the process of unfolding the divine plan of God. It simply set the stage for the next phase in the exercise of the will of God.

The earthly ministry of managing the Old Covenant had limitations and could not take the believer beyond a certain level and ultimately to perfection.[26]

We must, however, bear in mind that God emphatically instructed Moses to build the tabernacle according to the pattern. *"See that you make all things according to the pattern shown you on the mountain."*[27] In spite of the fact that it was built according to the pattern, it had deficiencies. The reason may be found in that it was merely a "model" (and not the original) and in that it was ceremonially managed by people impaired by sin. Moreover, from a prophetic standpoint, it was a precursor of that which was still to come. *"For the law appoints as high priests men who have weakness, but...."*[28] The priesthood religiously observed and maintained the system but was limited in taking their adherents any further in the quest for intimacy with God or perfection.

Another noteworthy point is that the Old Covenant models religion as a repetitious system that traditionally and religiously maintained the status quo of an order that could not take people beyond their limitations. It operated on a "maintenance" model. *"And every priest stands ministering daily and offering repeatedly the same sacrifices, which can never take away sins."*[29] It was a repe-

---

[26] Hebrews 8:7; 10:1.

[27] Hebrews 8:5.

[28] Hebrews 7:28.

[29] Hebrews 10:11.

titious system that mechanically followed the daily rituals that restricted access to the *"Holiest of All."* The adherents of the system could not be brought to the place of fullness or total harmony with their God.

Finally, the Old Covenant religious system was excessively hierarchical in its structure. It was maintained by a "classified group of priests" who had great powers of authority over the people. It profiled and distinguished an elite group from the rest of the people. The privileged few had "access" to God, thereby creating a dichotomy between clergy and laity. Consequently, the system produced dependence on this select group of people to represent the masses before God. Hence, entry into the presence of God was confined to the spiritually elite.

The New Covenant (New Testament)

The New Covenant illustrates the consummation of the divine agreements with humanity through the redemptive work of Jesus Christ. He became the surety of a better covenant that secured eternal redemption for humanity.

According to Hebrews,[30] the reformation of Jesus Christ did not only render the Old Covenant obsolete, but also heralded a new relationship with God. For example, the New Covenant internalised religion and caused the believer to focus on personal spiritual service. It introduced to the seeker the religion of the heart (internal religious system) that substituted the emphasis on external religious activity. The crux of the message reveals a personal, inward nature of religious fervour and not merely an external corporate system of worship. This does not, in any way, infer that external religious behaviour was no longer necessary. In

---

[30] Hebrews 9:10.

9

fact, it asserted that the religion of the heart should reflect itself dynamically through the lifestyle of the individual. The message and the messenger have to become one. An individual must preach that which he or she has already practised.

> *"This is the covenant that I will make with them after those days, says the Lord: I will put My laws into their hearts, and in their minds I will write them," then He adds, "Their sins and their lawless deeds I will remember no more"* (Hebrews 10:16-17).

This recommends that an old way of conducting ministry should be replaced by the changing of the personnel. Remember, at the point of the rending of the veil the entire priesthood became redundant, since the Old Covenant system of religion had become obsolete. At that point the priesthood was changed. In effect the change immediately graduated the believer into the office of priesthood.[31] Therefore, it was incumbent upon every believer to manage his or her own spiritual well-being and relationship with God. The wall of demarcation was dismantled and every person had direct access to God, through Jesus Christ.

Martin Luther: The 16th Century Reformation

Although it is not within the scope of this book to delve too deeply into theological discourses, it is at the same time prudent to make some reference to the great Reformation sparked by Martin Luther in the 16th century. Apart from the reformation of Jesus Christ, this will arguably be categorised as one of the most defining reformations in the history of humankind. In his pursuit

---

[31] Hebrews 7:12; 8:7-12; 10:16-17.

for spiritual satisfaction, Luther's discovery of the verses stating that *"the just shall live by faith"* and salvation by grace through faith caused the dam walls to burst and usher the Church into freedom from religious captivity.[32] Although he provoked great controversy and challenged the status quo in his day, his was a reformation of the theological content of the teachings and practices of the Church. This was an amazing reformation that changed the face of Europe and the world at large. Yet it did not bring a holistic reformation of every aspect of the substance and structure of the Church. It is within this backdrop that serious attention must be given to the Apostolic Reformation of the 21st century.

Apostolic Reformation and 21st Century Christianity

In the backdrop of what has been written, one has to come to the sad conclusion that a large segment of the Church has deviated from the blueprint of the New Covenant and is still living in the shadow of the past (the Old Covenant). The Church has degenerated to an old order that practises religion based on the norms of the Old Covenant. A great deal of emphasis is placed on external forms of religious expressions that are in opposition to the spirit of the New Covenant. These centres are maintained by a "priest craft" of individuals who are very similar in nature to the priests of the Old Covenant. These "priests" intercede on behalf of the masses, creating a culture of dependency. People have resigned themselves from approaching and drawing near to God. They are prisoners of religious activity and programmes that cannot satisfy their spiritual desires. Nevertheless, it must be stated categorically that, in the Apostolic Reformation, redefinition is brought to the ministry, place and function of the fivefold ministry in the New

---

[32] Hebrews 10:38; Ephesians 2:8.

Testament Church. Every effort ought to be made to submit to these ministry gifts, since they were positioned in the Church by the Lord Himself. These gifts play a critical role in the life of every believer, but they are not the priesthood of the Church. They are the skilled workers or craftsmen who are used to build the Church of Jesus Christ. Their role must be redefined and brought back to the correct place that was divinely intended for them.

I must also point out that corporate external religious expressions can be one of the noblest forms of worship, especially when it is in compliance with the internal state of believers who are sincerely walking in integrity before the Lord. The cry for reformation does not oppose ministry to people and the acquisition of buildings as venues for the assembling of the Church. However, it does confront and challenge any system of religion that focuses on the external forms of religion at the expense of the heart-issues of religion being left unquestioned. The passion of reformation is to bring the Church back to religious purity both individually and corporately.

In the Apostolic Reformation redefinition is brought to the religious practice of Christians. Critical analysis must not only be brought to the external structures of our worship services, but also to the quality of our internal lives that constitute the basis of true worship. In other words, the whole liturgy of the Church must be measured so that the substance of our worship (within our sacred buildings and outside) can be divinely accepted as being *"in spirit and truth."*[33] The picture of Zerubbabel measuring the finished building of the Temple is a prophetic type, highlighting the point that the completion of the building of the Church of Jesus Christ must be preceded by a critical evaluation

---

[33] John 4:24.

of the structure and content of the Church, thus ensuring that it is a perfect piece of work.

One of the critical areas of concern that reformation highlights is the inherent culture of corporate liturgy or worship prevalent in many congregations within the global Church. It would seem that worship has been relegated to a place of "entertainment" on a "sacred day" by a select group of charismatic and very skilled individuals. This is no different to the popular culture of the day where the demand for entertainment is a feature of contemporary society.

It is also interesting to observe that there are no set patterns laid out in the New Testament on how the worship service should be formatted. It seems that the gathering of the believers was more *organic* than *organised*; even though we read of their meetings being characterised by the breaking of bread, reading of the Scriptures, listening to the apostle's doctrines, singing, praying and ministering in the gifts and encouraging each other. Although all of these, and probably more, were encountered in their corporate times of fellowship, there was no fixed structure that one can conclusively point out in the early and developing New Testament Church. However, although this may be the case, it is worth noting that all references to worship[34] have a bearing on one's *personal* life and *not* on the *corporate* life of the Church. This is in sharp contrast to contemporary worship patterns that promote fixed external forms of worship. Without seeking to be overly critical, one cannot help but highlight the fact that these external forms of liturgy, such as performance and showmanship, conformity to current worldly fashions, the focus on popular groups and personalities and the appeal of rhythm, style and beat, are some of the features that

---

[34] Read Acts 16:25; Ephesians 5:19; 6:18; James 5:13.

preoccupy the attention of much of Christendom today. A careful study of David's life presents us with a model of a range of expressions in worship. A noteworthy aspect of the worship of his day was that it did not merely focus on the skill of the choir and musicians but on the Lord. The talent and giftedness of these worshippers did not divert attention away from the Lord. Nothing of flesh stood in the way of the Lord.

Apostolic Reformation: Definition of Religion

The Apostolic Reformation is a cry for pure religion to become the practice of the Church. It is evident throughout the Scriptures that religion that is *"pure and undefiled"* pleases God's heart. God is attracted to that which creates an environment that is in keeping with His holy nature. The word "pure" (Greek *katharos*) in the Epistle of James[35] has reference to religion that is clean and clear.[36] In it is found legal and ceremonial cleanliness that is free of pollution and the guilt of sin. Such religion does not produce any soil or stain. The adherents are not contaminated by the system.

The word "religion" (Greek *threskos*) conveys the idea of outward service to God; that is, the outward framework of religious activity. It is different to the word "godliness" (Greek *eusebeia*), the inward piety of the soul. However, pure religion is the expression of the organization of one's inward life that is governed by a deep piety and reverence for God. This is reflected in one's outward appearance and behaviour toward God and fellow humanity. Pure religion has nothing in it that defiles. It is that kind of system that is intrinsically clean and does not pollute people.

---

[35] James 1:27.

[36] S. Zodiates, ref. 2513, p. 1843.

Jesus launches a scathing attack on religious behaviour that violates the divine order:

> *These people draw near to Me with their mouth,*
> *and honor Me with their lips, but their heart is far*
> *from Me. And in **vain** they **worship** [my emphasis]*
> *Me, teaching as doctrines the commandments of men*
> (Matthew 15:8-9).

Christ states that worship that is not consistent with the divine requirement will be rendered groundless and futile because the hearts of the people are at a distance from the primary object of their worship. The word for "worship" (Greek *sebumai*) refers to bodily movement that expresses an attitude of respect by something great and lofty. Inferred in this is the thought of worship that is externally religious but no different to a cult, since the hearts of the people are inflated with selfish ideals and are not in tune with their external actions. He states that "*these people draw near to Me with their mouth…but their heart is far from Me.*"[37]

The Need for Reformation

The need for Reformation places a demand upon Church leaders to embrace the call to change and move to the place of biblical and spiritual exactness. It is against this backdrop that I have used Gilgal as a case study. It provides some of the principles that can guide the Church to the place of spiritual exactness. Gilgal is the place of **re-formation**. It is a signpost directing Church leaders to the fundamental principles for a successful and smooth biblical transition from an old season.

---

[37] Matthew 15:9.

Gilgal is not only a geographical place in the journey of God's people, but it also graphically depicts a strategic spiritual location in their journey. Places like Gilgal and others in the Old Testament became the "sacred places" of the Jews. At such places, memorials were erected to help future generations learn invaluable lessons that would guide them in their pilgrimage through life. Here at Gilgal a wealth of information may be gleaned and factored into the current spiritual journey of the Church of Jesus Christ. This is a place where the ancient landmarks of the patriarchal fathers are visibly enunciated. Lessons can be derived for all generations to learn from. At this place, the hearts of the fathers (past generations) and the children (present generation) can be joined and become unified in defining and continuing the purposes of God in the earth.

It is at Gilgal where Joshua's leadership experiences are revealed. We also discover the foundational principles for building according to the divine blueprint. In a broader context, these principles can be applied to any period of transition that a Church may go through. If and when applied, they can prevent error, heresy, schisms and many other misrepresentations from entering into the Church. In this respect, Gilgal can serve as a plumb line for leaders who do not want to experience the pain of failure and the frustration of rejection within their congregations.

CHAPTER 2

The Place of Re-formation

*Then the Lord said to Joshua, "This day I have **rolled** [my emphasis] away the reproach of Egypt from you." Therefore the name of the place is called Gilgal to this day (Joshua 5:9).*

The name "Gilgal" has no etymology attached to it. However, there is consensus that the name means "the circle or wheel."[38] The word could also refer to a "circle of stones." There is a play on the word whose root is the same as the verb "roll," thus giving rise to the meaning "rolled away."[39] It is obvious that the diversity of the meaning of "Gilgal" extends beyond the boundaries of literal interpretation.

---

[38] Joshua 4:19; 5:9.

[39] M. Tenney, *The Zondervan Pictorial Encyclopedia of the Bible* ,Vol. 2, p. 725.

Bible teachers helpfully point out that names in the Scriptures are reservoirs of spiritual truth and information. "Through the transposition of a name by borrowing, substitution and deviation the enquirer is introduced to a place beyond the boundaries of its literal meaning. It is here that we draw immense truths of great spiritual value. Often, names in the Scriptures are transformed from a noun to a metaphor."[40] They become the figures of speech through which a fountain of spiritual truths spring forth and are communicated in human concepts. Their intention is to take the student from something known to something unknown.

The name Gilgal is pregnant with meaning. It provides the forum for discourse with the wisdom and counsel of God's inspired Word. It is a significant spiritual place in the history of Israel. The venue of the divine encounter of Joshua is the result of the encampment being named Gilgal and becoming a memorial to the Israelites until *"this day."* When such unique encounters occur, places in life are named or renamed since they capture and communicate the purposes of God through that experience. This fact can be traced throughout the journey of the patriarchal fathers. Their encounter with their God at a specific point and space in time provoked a naming (or changing of the name) of the venue of their experience. These places eventually became "sacred places" in the religious experiences of the Jews.

Gilgal: Spiritual Application

In the Bible, Gilgal is the name given to several towns of uncertain location. However, the most important location was Joshua's encampment near the Jordan. It is known as the first resting place of the Israelites after they crossed the River Jordan, which was

---

[40] W. Van Gemeren, *Interpreting the Prophetic Word*, p. 74.

situated on the east border of the city of Jericho. It is impossible to fit all the Bible references of Gilgal to a single location. There are at least two to six cities with the same name. Interestingly, studies attempting to ascertain the exact geographical locale of the various places named Gilgal cannot be accurately and conclusively pointed out. However, the references to the various locations named Gilgal clearly highlight the key role the place called Gilgal played in the ethos of Israel. Undoubtedly, it had a profound impact on the spiritual and natural history of the nation.

Even the writings of the Prophets, Amos and Hosea, make reference to Gilgal.[41] Amos attributes a spiritual significance to the names Bethel and Gilgal. Interestingly, these two places also feature prominently in the ministry of Samuel and the installation of Saul as king.[42] Bethel (house of God) is probably a reference to a place of divine encounter. It is the place of revelation—the access point into the heavenly realm. Here at Bethel, Jacob, the patriarch, encountered the awesome presence of God and also accessed the revelation of God's will for himself and his posterity. The encounter was so great that he made a solemn commitment to build God a house in the earth.[43] By this, he wanted to capture this divine moment and bring others to a similar experience. In Jacobs' estimation, Bethel is the house of God and the gateway into the heavenly realm. Here, he also received the revelation of the covenant that God had previously entered into with his ancestors. At Bethel, God's intents and purposes are clearly revealed.

Just as Bethel is rich with meaning, so is Gilgal. When the Prophets make reference to it, they are alluding to the place of

---

[41] Amos 4:4; Hosea 4:15; 9:15; 12:11.

[42] 1 Samuel 10–13.

[43] Genesis 28:10-22.

19

strategic planning, preparation (even though at times it is the place where evil is designed and constructed) and implementation. Essentially, Gilgal is that place in one's spiritual journey where clear instruction is received so that the Kingdom of God can be strategically and meaningfully advanced in the earth. This is that place of reflection, meditation and consecration to build accurately.

Although it is not the purpose of this book to present a detailed study of Gilgal, a brief study will elucidate the principles gleaned from it. As has already been stated, the application of these principles can guide the Church through any difficult period of transition. In a spiritual sense, Gilgal is the encampment that the Church must dwell at before being inaugurated into the new season.

Gilgal: The Genesis of New Beginnings

Gilgal is the place of encampment and rest that signifies the conclusion of one interval in the journey and marks the beginning of another. The Israelites' route had reached a full "circle" or orbit, marking the end of a long season. Joshua and his people must camp in preparation for the next phase in the unfolding plan of God for their lives. It was here that God would prophetically reconfigure the mind of Israel by removing the shame, reproach and stigma of slavery, and "reconfigure" or "reprogramme" the nation so that it could be aligned to the demands of the new season.

Gilgal: The Strategic Centre of Divine Activity

As has been previously stated, Gilgal does not merely refer to a geographical location; it also symbolised a major spiritual place where a nation was being strategically developed. At this place, the Israelites were positioned, prepared and established for the advancement and fulfilment of the divine purpose in that specific phase of their journey. The significance of this place is evidenced by the influential role it played in the lives of leaders like Joshua, Saul, David, Elijah and Elisha. In a prophetic sense, it represented the stronghold of God in the earth. The Angel of the Lord, the principal power that supervised heaven's activity over Israel, was stationed at Gilgal:

> *Then the Angel of the Lord came up from Gilgal to Bochim…* (Judges 2:1).

Arguably, this verse suggests that Gilgal is the *command centre* of the Lord. From this "place" the Lord "watched" over the nation of Israel. It is evident that this was Joshua's base from which he launched his military expeditions. Most of his instructions from God were received at Gilgal. Even his strategy of conquest was developed and finetuned here. This was undoubtedly the nerve centre of a major part of his military campaigns into Canaan. Even the Prophet Elijah used Gilgal (near Jericho) as his head-quarters for ministry.[44] It was from here that he commenced a journey that eventually ushered him into Heaven.

Gilgal: Place of Instruction

An excellent example of Gilgal being a place of instruction is that of the sad story of the rise and fall from power of King Saul. After he was anointed by Samuel as king over Israel, Saul was instructed by the Prophet to go immediately to Gilgal and wait there for seven days, for further instructions concerning details

---

[44] 2 Kings 2:1; 4:38.

of his mandate and function as king over Israel.[45] The *set time* of instruction was seven days. The Hebrew word for "set time" (Hebrew *moed* or *moadah*) refers to an appointment or gathering.[46] Often it designates a determined time or place of meeting *without any regard for the purpose on hand.*[47] In other words, the appointment was more important than the necessity to prematurely address the needs of the nation, no matter how urgent they may be. The time set by Samuel was the time when Saul was to meet with God and receive his assignment as king over the Israelites Instead, he did not heed the instruction and only went to Gilgal two years later after he defeated the Ammonites.[48] It was only after the threat of a Philistine invasion that Saul observed the "seven day" appointment at Gilgal, but by then it was too late. He did not follow the process that would have led him to the throne. Actually, he took a shortcut to the throne without going through the period of reformation and reconstruction at Gilgal. Unfortunately, his place of instruction became the place of destruction. Here, he was dethroned as king over Israel. From that time on, Saul relocated his base from Gilgal to Gibeah.[49] The Scriptures do not record any other visit of Saul to Gilgal.

Saul's insensitivity in keeping the divine appointment can be a lesson for the Church today. He teaches us that no matter what the mandate of a new season in God may be or the urgency in disseminating it, there cannot be an activation of the divine assignment without the Church first coming to "Gilgal." Here

---

[45] 1 Samuel 10:8.

[46] 1 Samuel 13:8.

[47] S. Zodhiates, ref. 4150, p. 1626.

[48] 1 Samuel 11:14-15.

[49] 1 Samuel 13:15.

the Church must wait (seven days) until the Church fully understands the extent of the revelation of God for that new season. No matter what or how urgent the purpose is, the period of patiently receiving instruction must always precede any hasty dissemination of the mandate. It is regrettable that so many ministries are hurriedly dispensing the message of the new season without fully comprehending the mandate of the season. Unless the message is firmly incarnated in the life of an individual or a people, it cannot be communicated—the message must first become flesh and dwell among the people before it can be proclaimed to the nations. The message and the messenger must become one. We can all learn a lesson from the laws of nature that there cannot be the birth of anything without impregnation.

Gilgal: The Place of Re-formation

Gilgal is a place of re-formation. There can be no entry into the next season without the people of God arriving at a place of reconstruction. Here they are strategically positioned and prepared for the demands of a new season. Disobedience by refusing to acknowledge the Gilgal principle(s) can result in ministries being rendered idle or made obsolete to the purposes of God for that season.

Even David experienced the re-formation process at Gilgal. King David took refuge at Gilgal from his usurping son Absalom.[50] It was the bleakest point in his life and it seemed like his function as king of Israel was over. The tribe of Judah met him at Gilgal, and the process was set in place for the recovery of the kingdom. Here, they established a strategy for the

---

[50] 2 Samuel 19:15.

23

reestablishment of the kingdom from Absalom and the reinstatement of David as the king over the nation.

The Jordan Valley: The Place of Transition

The spiritual significance of Gilgal is further accentuated by our understanding of the Jordan Valley. Gilgal is the place *just beyond* the River Jordan. Without crossing the Jordan, one cannot come to a place called Gilgal. In a symbolic sense, the River Jordan is the place of *transition*. There cannot be any *re-formation* without going through the waters of transition.

The murky waters of transition are a period of serious preparation for the uncertain future. At such a place, an old season is terminated and buried and a new season is born. In this regard, Moses (at the River Jordan) makes use of the Law to prepare and condition the people for the journey ahead of them. At the Jordan, the Scriptures were interpreted and taught through the lenses of their impending prophetic destiny. Those aspects in the Word of God that could not have been seen in one's journey through the wilderness, was discovered through the prophetic lenses of divine revelation. Here, the focus of the people was adjusted and aligned to the divine will. They were mentally and spiritually prepared for a new leader, the demands of a new mandate and the challenges of the new landscape that lay ahead of them.

John the Baptist also used the Jordan Valley as a place to prepare the people of Israel for transition and the advent of a new religious order of life. Here, he became one of the most powerful voices crying in the wilderness for the people to prepare for a visitation of God. He also directed the people to a new leadership structure that was to supersede the existing system. Essentially, he prepared the nation for the unknown and for the One who would fulfil all things.

There can be no transition without a mentality or paradigm shift. At the Jordan, the mentalities and perspectives were changed. The wilderness mentality gave way to the urban mentality. The minds of the Israelites were reconfigured and the programme that once computed their pattern of thinking was altered. Their sight was set to see the future and thereby make the necessary preparations for that future in their present context.

Transition is not only a spiritually enlightening time, but also a dark and difficult time. At such a place, one has to let go of the familiar for the unfamiliar. The Jordan Valley is the lowest place in the earth, and by crossing the flooded Jordan one is descending to probably the lowest point in one's life. In a sense, it graphically portrays a picture of everything in one's life and ministry that has gone (or is going) wrong. This is the place of death—the place where old religious systems die and the paradigms of a previous order are dismantled.

In recent years, the Church has been going through a period of transition. When transition is implemented, there is the possibility of leadership changing. Moses understood that transition is preceded by the death of old mentalities and in many respects the necessity for the change of leadership. When he understood that his ministry was nearing an end, he gracefully prepared his people to receive Joshua as the new leader. He taught them to accept the changes that were to take place without departing from the way of the Lord. He probably understood that the new plan of God was a continuity of the old and he wisely used the Scriptures to reveal the continuing plan of God for their lives.

Most leaders are fearful of the new because they think that it is a gross disregard and rejection of the old. This is not necessarily a correct perception to adopt. The passing through the Jordan Valley, the place of transition, is actually not merely the venue where a new vision begins, but it is the continuation of the eternal vision in a new way. The predestined plan of God for the Church has never changed, but His *modus operandi* is always changing. It is important to remember that God builds "generationally." That is why He is referred to as the God of Abraham, Isaac and Jacob. Moses' leadership is commendable in that he not only built for the future generations of Israel but also that he recognised the time when his ministry was to be succeeded by Joshua. Consequently, at the appropriate time, he gracefully handed over the leadership reins to him.

Leaders must discern when their season in the divine programme is over and when to hand over the reins of responsibility to their successors. Even David, "a man after God's own heart." comes to a place in his life when he loses "heat"[51] and must apostolically install Solomon to the throne.

Presently, there are many churches in the Jordan Valley. There is the stirring of the "eagle's nest" and a desperate cry for change. The Prophets have declared the mind of God for this season and have encouraged the Church to make the necessary transition in preparation for a literal possessing of the divine promises. If people, churches and leaders do not change accordingly, they will be relegated to a place of total insignificance in the progressive plan of God in the earth and will inevitably die in the wilderness of barrenness.

The place immediately after navigating a difficult transition is Gilgal. Arguably, Gilgal refers to that spiritual place in the pilgrimage of God's people who have completed a "full cycle" or "orbit" in their journey. In the history of Israel, their journey began with 70 people who departed from the land of Canaan

––––––––––––––––

[51] 1 Kings 1:1 KJV.

during a time of famine. They lived in Egypt for over 400 years. Now they had returned to the place of their departure. At Gilgal, they were divinely repositioned and realigned before being launched into a new season in their pilgrimage.

Gilgal is not merely a place of rest but a place of restructuring—a place of re-formation. It symbolises a sensitive and serious place in the life and experience of a people, ministry or nation in the earth. This is a place, in the spirit, where a people must camp in preparation for the next phase in the unfolding plan of God for their lives. A season has been concluded and a new one is about to begin. God is placing new demands on His people. Here, the process of reconfiguration must take place.

CHAPTER 3

The Prophetic Reconfiguration of Mindset

Then the Lord said to Joshua, "This day I have rolled away the reproach of Egypt from you." Therefore the name of the place is called Gilgal to this day (Joshua 5: 9).

Gilgal represents a place at which the thought processes of a nation are shaped by the voice and will of God. One of the first things God does in preparing the nation of Israel for conquest is to "prophetically" reconfigure the perspective of their own identity and destiny. It is a re-formation of the structure of the thinking of Israel. At Gilgal, God unveils the desire and plan He has for the *Israelites*.

Gilgal is a defining moment in the history of Israel. It is at Gilgal that the Israelites were informed that a cycle in their journey was completed. Their negative historical past was adjusted and brought into alignment with their present and future destiny. The process of emancipation that commenced under the leadership of Moses was concluded under the leadership of Joshua. The "programme of reproach" that characterised the behaviour of the people of Israel in their journey from Egypt to the Promised Land was radically terminated.

A study of Israel's journey through the wilderness reveals the indelible impression that the sojourn in Egypt made on the Hebrew people. This may be understood in the light of the hardships and sufferings they had undergone for 400 years. The oppressive Egyptian system had made them slaves and marred their lives and identities. The *"reproach of Egypt"* was etched into the psyche of the Hebrews. After so many years of slavery, at Gilgal a new perspective of their future was divinely inscribed into their mindsets. Their present interpretation of life was no longer shaped by the bondage of their past experiences but by their renovated understanding of God and their destiny. By understanding their future, their prophetic lenses were aligned and adjusted so that they could transcend their past experiences and their temporary present reality and become *au fait* with the will of God for their lives. . The divine message radically changed the elevation of the people from that of oppression to progression as God's chosen nation.

The Prophetic Voice Is Directional

The prophetic word goes before a people and guides them into understanding the fullness of God's purposes for their lives. An example of this is the life and ministry of Timothy. The prophecies released to Timothy were the compass that shaped and directed his ministry as he steered his way through life.

> *This charge I commit to you, son Timothy, accord-*
> *ing to the prophecies previously made concerning*
> *you, that by them you may wage the good warfare*
> (1 Timothy 1:18).

The apostolic and prophetic release upon Timothy was to ensure that he functioned in his appointed place within the Body and that he clearly understood his duties. These instructions were received by prophetic impartation and apostolic "commanding." *"Previously made* [Greek *proago*[52]] *concerning you,"* makes reference to Timothy being led by the prophetic word released upon him at a specific time and place. It is evident that the apostolic charge or prophetic impartation directs and goes before those who are serving the purposes of God. These instructions help them to fight correctly and also guide them into fulfilling their function according to the divine intent. In fact, it was through the prophetic channel that he received the "gift":

> *Do not neglect the gift that is in you, which was given*
> *to you by prophecy with the laying on of the hands of*
> *the eldership* (1 Timothy 4:14).

The Prophetic Provides Spiritual Interpretation

A characteristic feature in prophetic ministry involves that of lending *spiritual interpretation*, especially in directing the Church in her journey. The prophetic office is the voice that interprets and thereby proclaims the mind of God to the people. This does not imply that the believer does not have the right to spiritual

---

[52] IS. Zodhiates, ref. 4254, *proago* – to go before or to lead.

interpretation. Although it is the privilege of every believer to know the mind and counsel of God, there is little questioning that the office of the Prophet encourages and sharpens the ability of the believer to know the mind of God personally and for the Church at that time in history.

Often the predictive (an integral aspect) in prophetic ministry features so prominently that there is a lack of emphasis on other aspects of prophetic ministry. The function of spiritual interpretation plays a fundamental role in the office of prophetic ministry. "It is the interpretation of everything from a spiritual standpoint; the bringing of the spiritual implications of things, past, present, and future, before the people of God, and giving them to understand the significance of things in their spiritual value and meaning."[53]

A key feature of changing seasons is the ability of Church leaders to interpret the will of God for that season. The function and nature of authentic prophetic ministry is evident in the life of Joshua. He was personally connected to the throne of God and directly received his mandate for the new season through the journey of the people. Joshua's communion with God ensured that he received guidance, direction and clarity of the mind and counsel of God. He had to interpret the will of God for the people. From this we can deduce that the interpretation of the message is fundamental to the application of that message.

At Gilgal, the will of God had to be *integrated* into the mentality of the people. Gilgal is that place where the leadership of the Church receives fresh directives from God. Leaders must not only hear a clear message from God, but also understand it so that the

---

[53] T. Sparks, *Prophetic Ministry, A Classic Study on the Nature of a Prophet* (Shippensburg, PA, USA: Destiny Image Publishers, 2000), p. 2.

people can be properly guided. Joshua had to receive firsthand instructions that were peculiar to his divine assignment. He could no longer walk in the shadow of the glory that he encountered when he served under the leadership of Moses.

The Prophetic Provides an Ear to Hear God

At Gilgal a forum of communication was established so that Joshua could receive a direct word from God. In every changing season there has to be the establishment of mechanisms to hear a clear word from God. A chronic problem in the Church is that it has cut off the prophetic voice from the congregation. Many Church leaders are occupied with doing things according to standards set by the systems of the world or by the traditions of the past. Although it can be argued that there is nothing wrong with learning from the world systems or from the traditions of the past, it must be emphasised that these "systems" cannot be the voice of God to Church leaders. Leaders must attune their ears to the voice of God and hear the mind of God for themselves and their people in any given season. When leaders fail to hear from God, they will become sceptical of changing seasons. For that reason, there will be opposition and insensitivity to God's unfolding plans.

Those who develop a listening ear to the voice of God will receive their divine assignments with all the divine resources and support to finish the work. These leaders become increasingly prophetic. They outpace their contemporaries. Their churches are progressive, vibrant and exude with excitement. They become pioneers and explorers of new frontiers in the Kingdom of God. As a result, they are often misunderstood, misinterpreted and misrepresented. Yet they can be consoled by the fact that there is vindication. God always justifies the faithful and He is true to His Word.

Prophetic Office in Fivefold Ministry

In this present season, God is restoring the office of the Prophet to its exact place and function within the fivefold ascension gift ministry.

> *And He Himself gave some to be apostles,* **some prophets** [my emphasis], *some evangelists, and some pastors and teachers* (Ephesians 4:11).

Jesus instituted five offices as unique resource centres for His Body. They were given for the benefit of the Church. Each of the fivefold ministry gifts is distinctive in that they are different to each other. However, they are all carriers of divine grace. Peter refers to the management of the manifold grace of God, or the many faces that the grace of God reflects.[54] In other words, the Disciples of Christ understood the administrative diversity of the fivefold ministry within the Body of Christ. They knew that the spiritual nature of the grace bestowed upon them defined, determined and computed their functioning within the fivefold ministry in the Body of Christ.

In this regard, the Prophet must be seen as a carrier of grace that is distinct from the other ascension gift ministries. The Prophet is carrying a grace that is a divine resource, an essential material for the building up of the believers. There is a spiritual technology in the office of the Prophet that contributes to the process of bringing the corporate Church to her complete and perfect stature in

---

[54] 1 Peter 4:10.

the earth. This office also helps the Church to stay connected to the "present truth" of God for His people within the context of their existence.

New Testament Prophets Defined

Presently the office and function of the Prophet and the prophetic ministry in general has been misunderstood and misrepresented. In some circles, this confusion is evident in the description of the ministry of the Prophet. They compare the ministry of the New Testament Prophet with that of the Old Testament Prophet. Although, in principle, these two functions are similar, there is a difference in the way they operate.[55] In the Old Testament the Prophet played a significant role in the history of Israel. In the New Testament, Christ chose Apostles to fill this role. This shows a break from the Old Testament times when the Prophet played a dominant and powerful role. In the New Testament, Apostles function prominently in the ministry of the Church, although the Prophets also play an integral part in the ministry of the Church. Connor asserts that the difference lies in the fact that "no New Testament Prophet was ever used in guidance and control of another person's life."[56] They were used to *confirm* the already known and revealed will of God. He purports that for the New Testament believers, "as many as are led by the Spirit of God, they are the sons of God."[57] "*To resort to a Prophet for direction, guidance and control, is to violate the ministry of New*

---

[55] Read K. Connor, *The Church in the New Testament*, p. 153-168 for a detailed description of the difference in the ministry of the Prophet in the Old and New Testaments.

[56] K. Connor, *The Church in the New Testament*, p. 166.

[57] Romans 8:14.

Covenant believers, of having access to God through Christ, by the Spirit, who is available for 'all flesh' in this dispensation.[58] He goes further to assert that they do offer to the Church the ministry of edification, exhortation and comfort so that the Church does not wander from the predetermined will of God.[59] In this sense, they bring validation to the purposes of God in the life of the Church.

While Connor highlights the difference between the prophetic office of the Old and New Testament, caution must be exercised in assuming that the Prophets in the new dispensation do not play a role in giving direction to the Church. As previously stated, the prophetic office does play a significant role in bringing interpretation and guidance to the Church, although it may not be as prominent as it was in Old Testament times. John the Baptist, as an inter-testament Prophet, proclaimed a message that gave direction and information to the advent of a new season emanating from the throne of God. He gave meaning to the processes of God in the earth. In Acts, prophecies were released to prepare the Church for the difficult times ahead of them. Paul was informed by the symbolic act of Agabus of his impending fate in Jerusalem:

> *When he had come to us, he took Paul's belt, bound his own hands and feet, and said, "Thus says the Holy Spirit, 'So shall the Jews at Jerusalem bind the man who owns this belt, and deliver him into the hands of the Gentiles'"* (Acts 21:11).

Agabus also prophesied about an impending famine in the world:

---

[58]   K. Connor, *The Church in the New Testament*, p. 166.

[59]   Ibid. Read 1 Corinthians 14:3 for further information.

> *And in these days prophets came from Jerusalem to Antioch. Then one of them, named Agabus, stood up and showed by the Spirit that there was going to be a great famine throughout all the world, which also happened in the days of Claudius Caesar* (Acts 11:27-28).

I am of the opinion that the office of the Prophet went beyond edification, exhortation and encouragement.[60] It also entailed direction (though not as prominent as the Old Testament Prophet), confirmation of divine actions, revelations, correction and judgment. However, when the Prophet releases directives to the Church, mechanisms should be in place to judge these and thereafter embrace the message. In this sense, the prophetic word must be judged and validated by the written Word. All revelation transmitted by the Prophet must be congruent with the Word of God. *In all cases, the ministry of the Prophet must illuminate the mind of the people with the will of God and bring them into a deeper relationship with their God.*

> *Let two or three prophets speak, and let the others judge. But if anything is revealed to another who sits by, let the first keep silent* (1 Corinthians 14:29-30).

The Purpose of New Testament Prophets

The primary objective of the office of the Prophet must be to *equip* every believer for the work of ministry. Prophets represent a foundational ministry in the Church, since they provide the framework of reference and patterns for accessing the mind

---

[60] 1 Corinthians 14:3.

of God. According to the Apostle James,[61] the Prophet always spoke in the name of the Lord. They spoke as the substitute or representative of the Lord. They were the mouthpiece of God; therefore, their behaviour had to conform to the character and purpose of God.

There are some who hold onto the "cessation theory"[62] that the office and function of the Prophet (and Apostle) is non-existent. They assert that the ministry of the Prophet (and Apostle) are temporary, transitional ministries that became inactive with the completion of the canon of New Testament Scripture. This theory is fraught with deficiencies and does not find authenticity in the Scriptures. In my opinion, the office of the Prophet (and Apostle) was given for the building of a complete or perfect Church. Therefore, these ministries cannot be rendered inactive without the Church reaching perfection. The cessation will only take place when the Church has *"come to the unity of the faith and of the knowledge of the Son of God, to a perfect man, to the measure of the stature of the fullness of Christ."*[63]

Essentially, the Prophet carries the unusual grace to receive messages that proceed directly from the heart of God.[64] The pres-

---

[61] James 5:10.

[62] Read Jon Ruthven, *On the Cessation of the Charismata*, *The Protestant Polemic on Postbiblical Miracles*, (Sheffield, England: Sheffield Academic Press, 1993), for a detailed Protestant assessment of the cessation theory.

[63] Ephesians 4:13.

[64] This view does not imply that Prophets are the only recipients of divine revelations or disclosures. Believers in general can function in the gift of prophecy even though there are boundaries to their ministry gift functions. A reading of Romans 12:6; 1 Corinthians 12:11; 14:1ff will assist in bring greater clarity to the gift of prophecy as distinct from the ascension gift of the office of a Prophet.

ence of authentic prophetic ministry releases into the atmosphere of the Church the grace to elicit messages from God. Whenever people are in the presence of a prophetic anointing and ministry, they are dynamically influenced into "prophetic behaviour." Even Saul, who was unskilled in prophetic ministry, immediately prophesied when he came into the environment of a prophetic company.[65] Prophets are God's technicians who erect satellite dishes, so that people can pick up clearer messages from the throne of God. The Prophets have the ability to climb mountains, study the movements of the heavens, engage in intimate communications with the Lord and then return to the people with a word from God. They have the gift to infect people, especially the uninitiated, with the capability to hear the voice of God for themselves and thereby know His will.

Churches and ministries cannot afford to cut themselves off from the office of the Prophet. It is my contention that it is the office of the Prophet that stimulates the believer to function in the gift of prophecy. This view does not in any way negate or restrict the ministry of the Holy Spirit, since every ministry in the Church is a gift of the Holy Spirit.

It is God's predetermined purpose that His people prophesy.[66] This implies that all His people understand and articulate His mind and counsel. In fact, it should be the natural ability of every Spirit-filled believer to prophesy.[67] Paul encourages the Church at Thessalonica not to *"despise prophecies."*[68] Even Moses expressed to Joshua the desire that all God's people should be Prophets:

---

[65]   1 Samuel 10:6.

[66]   Joel 2:28.

[67]   Acts 2:17-18.

[68]   1 Thessalonians 5:20.

Then Moses said to him, "Are you zealous for my sake?
Oh, that all the Lord's people were prophets and that
the Lord would put His Spirit upon them!"
(Numbers 11:29).

God has determined that His people walk in destiny and purpose by personally and corporately knowing His will for their
lives and that they are at all times in tune with the unfolding
revelation of the advancing Kingdom in the earth. God's people
must continuously be established in *"present truth."*[69] Prophets
are the technicians that assist in guiding people in accessing the
will of God for their lives. They feature prominently in teaching
people to hear the voice of God for themselves and not to create
a culture of dependency on the office of the Prophet for personal
direction and correction.

A congregation or ministry that accepts the prophetic office
and ministry will always desire to operate in the perfect will of
God. Moses mentored Joshua to always walk in obedience to God's
Word. It was in a "school of training" that Joshua received the grace
to walk in wisdom. He was *"full of the spirit of wisdom, for Moses*
had laid his hands on him."[70] At Gilgal, he captured the mind of
God because he was open to listening to the Lord. He received his
instructions directly from the Lord.

The Prophetic Word Shapes Mentalities

As already stated, the prophetic word communicated plays a
significant role in shaping the thinking of people. At Gilgal, the
mentality of the Israelites had to be reconditioned. They had to

---

[69] 2 Peter 1:12.

[70] Deuteronomy 34:9.

see themselves from within the context of the divine destiny for their lives. Their minds were scarred by memories of their negative experiences as slaves in Egypt. Their focus was on the past. The mentality of the people had to be divinely reconfigured. The reconstruction of the minds of people is a fundamental prerequisite to any move of God in the earth. Gilgal is that place of reconstruction. Yet there can be no true reconstruction of a people without a "rolling away" of the past reproach. It is these past embarrassments, failures, defeats, resentments, bitterness and other stumbling blocks that had to be removed before God could take the Israelites forward into His ultimate purpose.

The Prophetic in the Apostolic Reformation

In this season of the Apostolic Reformation, the spirit and grace of prophetic ministry places an urgent demand for the Church to accurately interpret the Word of the Lord. The sharpening of the perception of the mind of the Church cannot take place without the grace and anointing of prophetic ministry. This anointing has an unusual ability to bring people to understand the will of God for the present season. By giving the Church insight into the future, the entire behaviour of the Church is regulated. Perceptions change, vocabulary is refined or redefined and behavioural patterns are modified accordingly.

When people see into the plans of God, they desire to know how to participate in them. A very good application of this point is that of the Old Testament principle deduced from "spying out the land." For example, Moses was divinely instructed to select 12 spies from the 11 tribes of Israel and send them out to spy the land of Canaan.[71] In this story a divine principle is established:

---

[71] Numbers 13.

God cannot give His people anything (even though He is God) without first revealing it to them. After having seen what He desires to give them, they have the choice to either accept or reject His gift.

In its spiritual application, "spying out the land" is the prophetic ability of the Church to see into the predetermined will of God for their lives and thereby choose to collaborate with the divine intent or to reject it. Acceptance means adjustment and submission to the will of God. As a result, everything—mentally, physically and spiritually—must be adapted to the divine will. For this reason, it can be said that Prophets are like "spies" that catch sight of the mind of God and then prepare the Church for its unfolding revelation.

The prophetic spirit always precedes the conception or birthing of new things from Heaven. It is the voice that prepares the womb for the seed to be conceived. During the conception stage it oversees the growth process of the developing "seed" in the womb. After birth, it guides the developing baby until the will of God is activated into the earth. An example is that of the parents of John the Baptist, Zechariah and Elizabeth. They were prophetically chosen and prepared for the birth of one of the greatest men to have lived in the earth.[72] The disclosure of the will of God precedes the inauguration of His will. He first *announced* His plans to Zechariah before Elizabeth was impregnated. The prophetic revelation fully described the role that their son would play in redemptive history. They complied accordingly. Mary is another case study of one who was prepared for one of the most extraordinary experiences in history. As a virgin, Mary agreed to carry the divine seed in her womb, despite the negative social consequences.

---

[72]   Read Luke 1:5ff.

Elijah and John the Baptist present to the Church an excellent model of the role and function of prophetic ministry. They also communicate the spirit of the present Apostolic Reformation season. Both shared the similar grace configuration that gave expression to the call for reformation. They functioned at a crisis point in the history of religion—a time that was bankrupt of spiritual "things." Their grace and calling was to confront evil and erroneous religious systems that gave undiscerning followers an inaccurate definition of spirituality. The religious structures of their day were polluted by the mantic and magical practices of the pagans. Religion, in their time, involved the worship of many gods that adulterated the revelation of Yahweh.

Elijah is the beginning of the prophetic office of *covenant prosecutor* in the sense that he accused God's people of treachery and comforted the remnant with the hope of God's Kingdom. He brings a "prophetic lawsuit" of judgment against the king and the nation. They are charged with the failure to conform to covenant expectations.[73] Elijah shaped the course of the classical Prophets. The prophetic message of the classical Prophets includes a statement of God's legal suit against His people, an announcement of judgments, a call for repentance and a proclamation of the good news of God's deliverance. All the Prophets, from Elijah to John the Baptist, share a common message of judgment against the self-sufficient and of hope to all who longed for His Kingdom. They prayed for the people to repent and undergo a transformation by the spirit and to enjoy the blessings of the Kingdom. John the Baptist was the last segment of this prophetic stream.[74]

---

[73] 1 Kings 18:21.

[74] W. Van Gemeren, *Interpreting the Prophetic Word, An Interpretation to the Prophetic Literature of the Old Testament*, p. 28.

The divine mandate of both Elijah and John the Baptist was to "prepare the way." Both of them directed their message to the king (Ahab/Herod) and to the nation. They sought more than a cosmetic rearrangement; they sought to "uproot the tree," obliterate the system. The altar of Baal worship and its complex network of false prophets had to be completely annihilated. Elijah was entrusted with the responsibility of bringing down the "high places" of idolatry introduced by Jeroboam and perpetuated by Ahab and his wife Jezebel. John was responsible for announcing and preparing the mindsets of the people for one of the most revolutionary reformations to be experienced by Judaism. Both of these ministries arrive at a significant stage in God's dealing with humanity with a fresh mandate from the throne of God. Their ministries operate from the "wilderness" or "the Jordan." They are pivotal players in the divine arena entrusted with the responsibility of being the "bridge" for the people to cross the "Jordan" into a unique period of transition in both their spiritual and natural history. Both were responsible for taking the Church beyond the Laws of Moses. The thrust of their ministries transmit and invoke into the Kingdom of God a level of "violence" never before experienced in the unfolding purposes of God. The Prophet Isaiah provides an apt description of these two ministries and the anointing that configured them.

> *"Comfort, yes, comfort My people!" says your God.*
> *"Speak comfort to Jerusalem, and cry out to her, that*
> *her warfare is ended, that her iniquity is pardoned; for*
> *she has received from the Lord's hand double for all her*
> *sins."*

> *The voice of one crying in the wilderness: "Prepare*
> *the way of the Lord; make straight in the desert a*
> *highway for our God. Every valley shall be exalted and*
> *every mountain and hill brought low; the crooked places*
> *shall be made straight and the rough places smooth; the*
> *glory of the Lord shall be revealed, and all flesh shall*
> *see it together; for the mouth of the Lord has spoken"*
> (Isaiah 40:1-5).

The reformers' ministry emerges at a time and place in the life of a people that is filled with dearth, inertia and famine. They are intent on changing the operational system of the heart so that the purpose and conduct of the people will be perpetually "comforted." Speaking "comfort" (Hebrew *nacham*[75]) depicts the physical and spiritual state of the people. "Comfort" describes the physical display of one's inner feelings, usually "sorrow, a groan, to be sorry, or to breathe strongly." It conveys a change of heart or disposition; a change of purpose or a change in one's conduct. It is also translated as "repent" in many translations. The Reformers strive to bring comfort to the pain, discomfort and spiritual impoverishment of the people. They recognize the fact that only a change of the "heart" can bring about true comfort to the people. In this sense the "heart" is viewed as the internal operational system that configures, regulates and establishes the behavioural pattern of the religious system.

Thus the prophetic anointing targets the heart of religion. It addresses every inaccuracy with the hope of bringing people to a place of spiritual comfort. The primary motivation of the prophetic is to create a pathway for the return of the Lord Jesus

---

[75] S. Zodhiates, ref. 5162, p. 1635.

Christ in and to His Church. They often work in the wilderness of barrenness and isolation—they are the "voices crying in the wilderness." For this reason it can be asserted that the prophetic always precedes the apostolic ministry. In the Apostolic Reformation, the grace of this dynamic dimension of prophetic ministry is visibly evident. It is comparative with the prophetic declaration that the "Lord will send the spirit of Elijah".[76] Many who are heralding the Apostolic Reformation portray strong traits of the spirit of Elijah. They are contributing to the programme of building bridges, fostering the spirit of fatherhood and promoting a culture of equality in the Church. These are standing in various places in society and are confronting inaccurate and unbiblical practices in the Church and society.

---

[76] Malachi 4:5,6

CHAPTER 4

The Establishment of an Apostolic People

And it came to pass, when all the people had completely crossed over the Jordan that the Lord spoke to Joshua, saying: "Take for yourselves twelve men from the people, one man from every tribe, and command them, saying, 'Take for yourselves twelve stones from here, out of the midst of the Jordan, from the place where the priests' feet stood firm. You shall carry them over with you and leave them in the lodging place where you lodge tonight.'" Then Joshua called the twelve men whom he had appointed from the children of Israel, one man from every tribe; and Joshua said to them: "Cross over before the ark of the Lord your God into the midst of the Jordan, and each one of you take up a stone on his shoulder, according to the number of the tribes of the children of Israel, that this may be a sign among you when your children ask in time to come, saying, 'What

*do these stones mean to you?' Then you shall answer
them that the waters of the Jordan were cut off before
the ark of the covenant of the Lord; when it crossed over
the Jordan, the waters of the Jordan were cut off. And
these stones shall be for a memorial to the children of
Israel forever." And the children of Israel did so, just as
Joshua commanded, and took up twelve stones from the
midst of the Jordan, as the Lord had spoken to Joshua,
according to the number of the tribes of the children
of Israel, and carried them over with them to the place
where they lodged, and laid them down there. Then
Joshua set up twelve stones in the midst of the Jordan,
in the place where the feet of the priests who bore the
ark of the covenant stood; and they are there to this day*
(Joshua 4:1-9).

Twelve men, each a representative or leader of the tribes of
Israel, had taken 12 stones from the riverbed of the Jordan and
laid them at Gilgal. This symbolic act served as a memorial that
narrated the story to the future Israelite generations of how God
brought their fathers across the River Jordan to establish them as
a sovereign nation in a foreign land. The 12 stones, in all probability, typified and pointed to the formation of a "special" people
in the earth that was to be sanctified and governed by a divine
constitution.[77] By God building a new nation in the earth, He
will establish His righteous Kingdom and bring all things back
to Himself. The 12 stones laid by the 12 men set the pattern for
future generations to study how God builds His purposes into
the earth. In this regard, Gilgal can teach the Church many prin-

---

[77] Exodus 19:5.

ciples that are applicable to our understanding of the nature and function of apostolic ministry.

Before we explore the ministry of Apostles (and apostolic people), there are certain observations gleaned at Gilgal that will provide valuable insight into an understanding of the present season that the Church is encountering.

Firstly, the 12 men were instructed to go into the Jordan and remove the 12 stones only *after all* the people had *completely* crossed the river.[78] Implicit in this is the notion that all the people had to first cross over or *transition* into the new dispensation before the stones could be taken out of the Jordan. In other words, the building process could only be initiated after the entire nation had transitioned into the new season. It is apparent that nothing can be built during a time of flood or in a period of transition. The laying of foundations in the life of the Church can only take place after the difficult process of transition has been completed.

Secondly, the selection of a representative from each tribe was an indication of the *unity* of the tribes. It reflected the harmonious working together of the 12 tribes under the command of God in very testing circumstances (flooded river), by taking the stones out of the Jordan and placing them at their lodging place. From this, we can assume that oneness was, undoubtedly, an important requirement in the process of preparation for what lay ahead for the nation. This emphatically alludes to the fact that a divided people will be a hindrance to the effective implementation of the divine intentions in any given season. There is no doubt, in my mind, that disunity retards the momentum of God's will unfolding in the earth. However, apostolic ministry, as exhibited by the

---

[78] Joshua 4:1.

12 men, demonstrates the team spirit needed for synergistically building the purposes of God in the earth.

Thirdly, the *stones* were taken from the place where *"the priests' feet stood firm."*[79] It will seem likely that the same stones on which the priest had steadfastly stood upon were taken out of the turbulent and flooded Jordan to serve as a memorial to the future generations of Israel. By this, we can deduce that the stones that provided a firm foundation for the priests to stand upon and carry the Ark of the Covenant in a flooded river were to become the "type" of a foundation that will be used to build the people of God in the earth. From this point emerges the testimony that *"the waters of the Jordan were cut off before the ark of the covenant of the Lord; when it crossed over the Jordan, the waters of the Jordan were cut off. And these stones shall be for a memorial to the children of Israel forever."*[80] For all intents and purposes, it can be asserted that the principles of God are carried on the shoulders of those sanctified individuals who have founded their lives on the rock of His Word. It is these proven principles that have endured the tests of life that will be the foundation upon which the nation of God will be built. Apostles bring these principles to the Church of Jesus Christ.

Spiritual Significance of the Number 12

One cannot study the Scriptures without arriving at the viewpoint that there are consistent uses of numbers that convey spiritual truths. Connor aptly asserts, "God is indeed the wonderful *numberer* and we need to understand His use of numbers."[81]

---

[79] Joshua 4:3.

[80] Joshua 4:7.

[81] K. Connor, *Interpreting the Book of Revelation*, p. 164.

However, a student must be advised to cautiously make every attempt to stay within the boundaries of a judicious use of numbers when interpreting the Scriptures.

Nonetheless, at Gilgal it is evident that the choice of the 12 men carrying the 12 stones communicates a divine principle that will almost certainly unveil its fullest meaning in the New Testament. In this number is found the future function and ministry of Apostles (and apostolic ministry) in the Church. The number "12" is a symbol for government, authority and apostolic fullness.[82] It features prominently in the nation of Israel's redemptive history and in the prophetic references to the New Jerusalem, the city of God (Revelation 21–22).[83] The many allusions to the number 12 *symbolically* point to the structure of foundational ministries in the Church, the order or government of God in His Kingdom and His sovereign authority in creation. Furthermore, this principle is accentuated in the appointment, by Jesus, of the 12 Apostles. Although little background information is given to these individuals in the whole of the New Testament Scriptures, the tradition of the 12 is consistently emphasised and maintained. From this we can deduct the point of view that the *persons* in the 12 were not as prominent as the *principle* that the number 12 alluded to. A detailed study of the 12 Apostles will reveal that they functioned in relative obscurity. Little information is provided by the Scriptures about them or their exact ministries after the Ascension of Jesus. It would seem that while there was consistent reference to the 12, the details of each of the 12 was not as significant. Thus the view is communicated that there

---

[82] K. Connor, *The Church in the New Testament*, p.141.

[83] Ibid. Kevin J. Connor extensively defines the ministry of the Apostle and the significance of the number 12 in the Scriptures.

was an attempt to preserve the tradition of the 12 more than preserving the identity of each of them. The emphasis was not on the persons but on the symbolic meaning of the principle, represented by the number "12." In this regard it can be asserted that the principle of the 12 was significant in communicating the idea of divine government (or structure) to all that God constructs (or constructed) in the earth.

For this reason it can be argued that the apostolic is directly connected to a specific design, pattern and order that must be divinely established in the earth. I refer to this principle as building *apostolically*—that is, leaders (or people) who are commissioned by the Lord with the mandate to build strictly according to the revealed heavenly pattern. They are under the authority of the "sender" and cannot deviate from the original plan. Thus there cannot be an amendment to this plan.

The Old Testament teems with examples of people building apostolically. Noah built the ark according to the heavenly design.[84] Moses meticulously followed the comprehensive instructions of the Lord in the building of the tabernacle and the elaborate religious system of Judaism.[85] Solomon carefully followed the written plans handed down to him by his father David.[86] Even Elijah adopted the apostolic principle when rebuilding the altar by laying the 12 stones.[87]

Evidently, the various building programmes recorded in the Old Testament are shadows and types pointing to the "nation," "city" and "people" that the Holy Spirit is building through the

---

[84] Genesis 6:22.

[85] Exodus 25:40; Hebrews 8:5.

[86] 1 Chronicles 22:5ff; 1 Chronicles 28:11-19.

[87] 1 Kings 18:31.

sacrificial work of Jesus Christ in the earth. The message of the Apostolic Reformation calls upon fivefold ministers to build God's House according to the "pattern." The Prophet Ezekiel was instructed to describe the pattern to his people for the building of God's eternal dwelling place.

> *Son of man, describe the temple* [house] *to the house of Israel, that they may be ashamed of their iniquities; and let them measure the pattern. And if they are ashamed of all that they have done, make known to them the design of the temple* [house] *and its arrangement, its exits and its entrances, its entire design and all its ordinances, and perform them* (Ezekiel 43:10-11).

Apostolic Ministry Defined

The office of the Apostle (as that of all the fivefold ministry graces) was divinely instituted by Jesus Christ for the benefit of His Church.[88] These fivefold graces (Greek *domata*[89]) are actually a reflection of the nature of the gift (Christ) to His Body (the Church). In a technical sense, the fivefold graces reveal the "material" gifts given for the needs of the Church. It is in this regard that the office of the Apostle must be viewed as possessing a special endowment of grace (as will the rest of the fivefold graces) for a specific function within the Body of Christ. However, it must be stated that Christ did not institute a hierarchical system of ministry but categories of authority to act as bond servants on His behalf for the building of His people in the earth. The ministry of Apostles not only establishes a representative authority but

---

[88] Ephesians 4:7-16.

[89] Ephesians 4:7-8.

also actually brings Christ to the Church. Rejection of those sent by Christ is tantamount to rejection of Christ Himself:[90]

> *He who receives you receives Me, and he who receives Me receives Him who sent Me* (Matthew 10:40).

The Greek word used for Apostle in the New Testament is *apostolos*. It conveys the following meaning: "one sent forth" or "to act as an ambassador or messenger."[91] These are commissioned messengers carrying a specific message or mandate from their king. Perhaps the closest definition for Apostle in the Old Testament that amplifies the New Testament definition is *mal'akh.*[92] It refers to someone who has been dispatched as a deputy, a messenger or a herald. In the Old Testament, when God is doing the sending, it (*mal'akh*) may refer to an angel, a Prophet, a priest or a Teacher. In a general sense it often refers to an ambassador, representing the sender, in official negotiations or on some specific mission. Another parallel word for *apostolos* can be found in the rabbinic term *shaliah*. Both share the same meaning. In the circle of the Rabbis', it is said that "a man's agent is like to himself" and that the agent's acts implicate the principal.[93]

From this definition, we can deduce that the ministry of an Apostle is governed by a unique relationship with the sender and is enslaved to the will and desire of the one who sends. The office of the Apostle is distinctively disclosed. They have been

---

[90] Luke 10:10-12.

[91] S. Zodhiates. ref. 652, p. 238.

[92] S. Zodhiates. ref. 4397, p. 1741.

[93] C. Barrett, *The Signs of an Apostle*. The Cato Lecture 1969, p. 13.

uniquely appropriated to Christ so as to represent Him in their own person. In this regard, it can be asserted that they act in the person of the Lord Himself. Therefore, the Apostles' dignity and worth did not lie in themselves but in the one who sends. True Apostles do not place their personal agendas and ambitions above their master. They renounce the right to self-determination and commit to the course of their God. Their message and actions are bound up in each other, thus they enjoy and exercise great authority.

Apostolic Ministry Expounded

The 12 men who carried the stones from the river bring to light the significant role that the ministry of Apostles play in the birth, growth and establishment of the Church. Gilgal teaches us that 12 men were "prepared" before the implementation of the purpose of God in the earth. From this we learn that God uses people to fulfil or implement His purposes in the earth.[94] Jesus said that He "will build His Church," but the simple fact is that He employs people to build.[95] At the inception of Jesus' ministry, there was a selective process adopted that led to the choosing of the 12 who will become His Apostles and builders of His Church.

Presently, the global Church is witnessing the emergence of Apostles who are bringing, out of the Jordan, the foundational principles and strategies for building a new nation in the earth. In them are found the grace of wise master builders who will humbly teach and guide people in building correctly. They are the oracles sent from God who bring, to the Church, the stones of fresh

---

[94] 1 Corinthians 3:9.

[95] Matthew 16:18.

revelations, which are the ancient landmarks established before the foundations of the earth. According to Paul, the Apostles and Prophets have been endowed with grace to decode the mysteries that have been concealed from previous generations.[96] They have the responsibility of bringing illumination to the Church concerning the will and counsel of God. They protectively ensure that strict biblical procedures are executed in the construction of God's house.

Kevin Connor asserts that in the last days there will be a visible witness of thousands of Apostles in the earth who will be modelled after the ministry pattern of Paul. These Apostles will have the "character, qualifications, revelation and ministry that Paul had."[97]

> *There is a theoretical teaching that in the last days, the Church will again be led by twelve Apostles, one of whom will "fall away" (like Reuben of the 12 sons, and Judas of the 12 Apostles) to become the last day antichrist. Such an apostolic college would be composed of Gentile Apostles of various races. Such teaching is based upon the symbolism of the 12 stars crowning the last day church (Revelation 12), and the meaning of the 24 elders of Revelation (12 early day and 12 last day Apostles). Obviously, we need thousands of Apostles to complete the perfection of the church and the evangelization of the world. But it is also great and very exciting to contemplate that just as the church age began with 12 Jewish Apostles leading a basically Jewish*

---

[96] Ephesians 3:5.

[97] K. Connor, *The New Testament Church*, pp. 145-146.

Church, The Age will end with 12 (or a representative number of) Gentile Apostles leading a mainly Gentile Church. Such Apostles would be a very special category of their own, and could only be brought together by God Himself.[98]

Although what Kevin Connor states opens the door to debate, one cannot help but recognise the wretched state of the Church and the need for authentic apostolic ministry to restore divine order among God's people. Arguably, the absence of Apostles in ministries and congregations is possibly one of the reasons for the inaccurate and dysfunctional state of the global Church. History abounds with examples of strange types of buildings that have distorted the picture of the perfect building that God has pre-determined for His dwelling place. One must ask the question as to whether the main reason for the erroneous patterns and designs are because of the absence of the grace of the Apostle in the Church. If we follow the pattern of the Scriptures, then we must assume that, without the grace of the Apostle, there will always be confusion raging over the exact nature of the details of the plan of God for His house. It is, therefore, of fundamental necessity that leaders of congregations identify the grace of the Apostle in the Church at large and establish covenantal relationship with Apostles so that they could be beneficial to the local congregation.

Apostolic Pillars

There is a prophetic statement communicated by the 12 men who, apart from carrying the 12 stones out of the Jordan, also

---

[98] Iibid.

took 12 stones from Gilgal and placed them in the Jordan. By this action, they were pointing to a future governmental order that was to be divinely established. These "stones" transmit a clear picture to the New Testament Church of a future order where God will build a new nation in the earth that will conform to the image of Christ. Peter refers to these people as *"living stones"* being constructed into a spiritual house that will offer up spiritual sacrifices acceptable to God through Jesus Christ.[99]

God explicitly instructs His servants to build altars, cities and the temple using hewn stones. There are many scriptural allusions to the use of stones. Even the Temple of Solomon was built with stones finished at the quarry.[100] Moses stated that the Laws were inscribed upon the 12 stones.[101] The stones epitomize the 12 tribes of Israel. On these stones, the constitution of God mirrored the divine laws that governed the entire Jewish nation. The principles of these laws were to assist the people to conform to a heavenly way of living.

In the Old Testament, there are many examples of God's methodology of building. One such example is that God builds His house by first cutting out His pillars. In Proverbs, it is clearly stated that wisdom builds the house by cutting her pillars:

> *Wisdom has built her house, she has hewn out her seven pillars* (Proverbs 9:1).

The stone that Jacob used as a *pillow,* which later was anointed with oil and called a *pillar,* is one of the most prophetic types,

---

[99]   1 Peter 2:5.

[100]   1 Kings 6:7.

[101]   Deuteronomy 27:1ff.

highlighting the significant role that pillars play in the Scriptures and in the building of God's house.[102]

> *And this stone which I have set as a **pillar** [my emphasis] shall be God's house, and of all that You give me I will surely give a tenth to You* (Genesis 28:22).

In all probability, this is the reference that Jesus made when He declared that *"on this rock I will build My church."*[103] It is, therefore, evident that God builds His Church with pillars and stones.

The Hebrew word *matstsebah,* for pillar, indicates "something that is stationed, set up or erected."[104] The root (Hebrew *natsab*) to this word is associated with the idea of stationing something or someone in a specific place. It portrays various postures of standing, often in positions of authority. In Psalms, this word (*natsab*) even describes God standing in the congregation.[105] From these words we can assume that God, through people He stations in strategic places in the Church, is Himself standing in a position of authority over His Church. In other words, it can be said that God stands in His house through the people He places in various postures of ministry.

Contemporary Church leaders must take cognisance of the principle extracted from this example: *There cannot be the implementation of a new order or structure in their congregations without their first seeking to identify and develop the people who will be the pillars in the congregation.* These pillars will keep the "building"

---

[102] Genesis 28:18-22.

[103] Matthew 16:18.

[104] S. Zodhiates, ref. 4676 & 5324, p. 1743.

[105] Psalm 82:1.

from falling during testing times. Many leaders impulsively intro-duce new structures into their congregations without realising that people are the structure of God's building programme. It is, therefore, imperative for leaders *to build people* and not only programmes maintained by people. These are the people who have been taken out of the Jordan and have been shaped by the creative hand of the Lord. They reflect the inscribed Word of the Lord on the tablets of their heart and have thus become the Word of the Lord for the new season.

The 12 Apostles were His pillars.[106] They shouldered the bur-den of the Lord for His Church. Pillars are a symbolic way of describing the manner in which God has chosen to stand in the midst of His people. *God stands in the congregation through pillars.* Therefore, leaders must fulfil their assignments by identifying those individuals who carry the anointing to be the pillars in the different ministries in the congregation. Even Jesus cut out His pillars, the 12 Apostles, before building His Church. *Leaders must follow this example by initially selecting their pillars before seeking to build their congregations.* Such individuals must have the oil of anointing upon them to fulfil their responsibilities in the con-gregation. They cannot be novices or individuals who are easily swayed by the challenges they may face.

One of the ways of selecting them is by identifying whether they are truly sons (disciples) of the one who leads them. Timo-thy was a true son of Paul, in that he could be entrusted with the responsibility and care of the Church at Ephesus. Paul knew that he would not deviate from that which he was apostolically and prophetically commissioned to do. In essence, pillars are often the spiritual sons of the leader in that they carry and reflect the seed

---

[106] Galatians 2:9.

of the father (the seed is the vision of the Lord for His Church within a specific context). Sons reflect the image and character of their spiritual father. A godly leader will know his sons by the seed they carry. Even the great king David developed and established his kingdom around his sons.[107]

These pillars uphold the Temple of God. If there are no pillars, then the building will falter and fall. Samson highlights this point when he musters up all his strength to bring down the pillars of the Philistine temple, consequently destroying the Philistine lords and the people in the temple.[108] To produce such pillars in the local congregation involves a serious endeavour to mentor people. There are possibly many programmes that can develop people, but I would like to suggest three programmes: *revelational, relational* and *generational.*

The *revelational* process of mentoring is connected to the full disclosure of everything one receives directly from the Lord. It is the transmission of all the revelation of God for the ministry. Leaders must expose, to their sons, everything that they have received directly from the Lord. There must be nothing hidden.

The *relational* approach is a practical outworking of ministry presented by a lifestyle that can be emulated. Leaders must demonstrate to their sons an example that will be desirously pursued. Their message must be compliant with their lifestyle.

Generational building involves the patriarchal practice of imparting and transferring responsibility for continuity of the divine purpose in the earth. In it lies the fluent passing on of the baton to a generation that will faithfully preserve the will of God in the earth.

---

[107] 1 Chronicles18:17.

[108] Judges 16:28-30.

Apostolic Foundations

By laying the 12 stones in the camp, the nation of Israel were establishing a divine principle for future generations to follow. They were communicating an apostolic principle for building: *Whatever God builds is built on a solid foundation.* The house that God is constructing is fixed on Christ, the firm foundation. Jesus stated that He will build His Church upon the *"rock"* of Peter's confession. By Peter declaring that *"You are the Christ, the Son of the living God,"* a statement by revelation was made confessing that Christ, the Logos, was the incarnation of God.[109] Literally, this inferred that the Church of Jesus Christ will be founded upon the Word of Peter's confession, i.e. upon the immovable Word. Upon this tried and tested precious foundation stone, the Temple of God will be built.

A defining feature of the ministry of Apostles (and Prophets) in the New Testament is associated with "foundations":

> *Having been built on the foundation of the apostles and prophets, Jesus Christ Himself being the chief corner stone* (Ephesians 2:20).

This verse can be interpreted in different ways with each interpretation communicating important truths. This statement embodies the salient truth that the messages of true Apostles are at all times Christocentric (Christ-centred). Essentially, Christ is the foundation upon which they build the foundation of the Church. Apostles who are sent from God do not preach anything else but the gospel of Christ and His Kingdom.[110] They do not

---

[109] Matthew 16:16-18.

[110] 2 Corinthians 11:4; Galatians 1:8-9.

draw attention to themselves, but to the one who sends them. If any Apostle draws attention to self, then such an individual is definitely not sent from God but seeks personal glory. The credentials of authentic apostolic ministry do not only seek to exalt and glorify God, but also demonstrate a lifestyle of truthful and righteous living.[111]

Furthermore, this verse does not imply that Apostles and Prophets lay foundations as in the traditional concept of church planting, unlike the view held by many in missiological circles. It is quite evident in the New Testament that not all Apostles (or Prophets) had founded churches. However, it is clear that all of them played an integral role in establishing the believers and congregations in the foundational principles, doctrines and truths of the New Covenant. They laid the substructure of the building so that the superstructure could be built. It would, therefore, appear that the ministry of the Apostles was to establish the fundamental principles in the operational system of the believer's mind so that, when activated, those principles will regulate and guide them in living for Christ. Paul states that he built as a wise master builder; he *"laid the foundation, and another builds on it"*:

> *According to the grace of God which was given to me, as a wise master builder I have laid the foundation, and another builds on it. But let each one take heed how he builds on it* (1 Corinthians 3:10).

Paul's travels expose the method he employed in establishing the believers. This involved the function of "confirming" or strengthening congregations in the faith. He did this by evaluating

---

[111] John 7:16-18.

their strengths and weaknesses, then ministering to them accordingly. Any inaccurate "foundation" was exposed and dealt with.

From another perspective, Apostles are spiritually endowed with the grace or ability to lay foundational (or the elementary) principles of the faith into the heart of the believer. They have this unique grace to plant the "seed" of God's word in the womb of the believer so that when it is conceived it will bring forth Christ. The 12 stones refer to the principles of God's Word being installed into the heart of the believer. In them is found the wisdom and counsel of God that regulates and influences the lifestyle of the believer.

Apostolic Wisdom

Another significant characteristic of apostolic ministry is the use of wisdom as the "master craftsman" in building the purposes of God in the earth. Fivefold leaders are encouraged to engage Wisdom as the principal craftsman in their building programmes. Wisdom builds the house.[112] Wisdom played an active and integral role in the creation of all things.[113] Wisdom is the "principal thing" in any building programme of God. The builders of God must build under the guidance and supervision of Wisdom. The intricate detail of God's designs and witty inventions can only be accessed through Wisdom.[114] The builders, employed to build the Tabernacle of Moses, were endued with great wisdom. They were skilled craftsmen, specialists in various fields of expertise related to the divine requirements. In Zechariah, we are provided with

---

[112] Proverbs 9:1.

[113] Proverbs 8:30.

[114] Proverbs 8:12.

an apt definition of *"craftsmen."*[115] They are highly skilled workers employed for a diversity of specialised tasks in the construction of the people of God. In the New Testament, Apostles are described as skilled craftsmen who have the anointing of a *"wise master builder."*[116] Their grace configuration is to carry the laws of God and to install them into the lives of people so that their lives will reflect the image of Christ in the earth. Paul's ministry is an excellent example of a craftsman who focused on building God's house in the earth.

Those in the fivefold ministry must focus on "building people" and not their own programmes and "churches." Church leaders must recognise each member of their congregation as a "living stone" who constitutes the superstructure of the house of God in the earth. There has to be a shift from merely focusing on building a large congregation that is no different from a crowd of people. Value has got to be brought back to every single member of the congregation. The emphasis ought to be directed on how each "living stone" can be prepared by the hammer of God's Word and then strategically placed in his or her ministry function and calling within the Body of Christ. The Church must be moved from Ai (a heap of stones) to Bethel (a house of God made up of stones).

The Apostolic Reformation postulates that this is the season in which God is restoring the grace of the Apostle back to its correct position in the Church. Through apostolic ministry, the measuring line is set to measure the house being built for Him. God uses Apostles to measure His house, thereby bringing it back to its original design. The ultimate objective of the divine will

---

[115] Zechariah 1:20-22.

[116] 1 Corinthians 3:10.

is to bring the fullness of Christ to the Church. Apostles play a fundamental role in conveying a unique endowment of grace to the Church. They do this by endeavouring to accurately build Christ into every believer. If a congregation does not have a resident Apostle in the people's midst, then they must make every attempt to identify and relate to this ministry gift from the larger Body of Christ. In so doing they will not rob themselves of this grace and will thereby enjoy the benefit of ensuring that they are building correctly.

We have learned from our study of Gilgal that chosen men were prepared to carry the stones from the River Jordan and set them as a memorial in the camp. In this season, people from total obscurity are being raised by the Spirit of God with apostolic grace to guide the process of building a "perfect man" in the earth.

CHAPTER 5

The Place of Circumcision

At that time the Lord said to Joshua, "Make flint knives for yourself, and circumcise the sons of Israel again the second time." So Joshua made flint knives for himself, and circumcised the sons of Israel at the hill of the foreskins. And this is the reason why Joshua circumcised them: All the people who came out of Egypt who were males, all the men of war, had died in the wilderness on the way, after they had come out of Egypt. For all the people who came out had been circumcised, but all the people born in the wilderness, on the way as they came out of Egypt, had not been circumcised. For the children of Israel walked forty years in the wilderness, till all the people who were men of war, who came out of Egypt, were consumed, because they did not obey the voice of the Lord—to whom the Lord swore that He would not show them the land which the Lord had sworn to

*their fathers that He would give us, "a land flowing
with milk and honey." Then Joshua circumcised their
sons whom He raised up in their place; for they were
uncircumcised, because they had not been circumcised
on the way. So it was, when they had finished
circumcising all the people, that they stayed in their
places in the camp till they were healed* (Joshua 5:2-8).

Gilgal is the scene and venue where God instructed Joshua to circumcise the nation of Israel for the second time. A whole generation
of uncircumcised Israelites, who were born in the wilderness, had
to undergo the painful process of circumcision, thereby affirming
their corporate identity as the nation of God. The Scriptures clearly
state that the generation that left Egypt was circumcised, but the
generation that was born in the wilderness was not. By the process
of circumcision, they were cutting off with "knives of stone" the
"unclean," since only a "circumcised" people could fulfil the purpose
of God. Thus, the old nature was "rolled" away and they dedicated
their lives to God and to His unfolding purposes.

Inferred in this procedure is the idea that an uncircumcised
nation could not begin the process of a systematic conquest of the
land of Canaan without first observing, affirming and reflecting
on the requirements of the covenant entered into between God
and its patriarch, Abraham. The significance of the rite of circumcision is accentuated by the demand on Joshua to circumcise
the people at such an unseemly place like Gilgal. It would appear
that this place of reconstruction had to be the same venue for
the consecration and the renewal of the Covenant, depicting a
nation that lived by a divine constitution. In a spiritual sense, the
"sons" of Israel who were circumcised a "second time" depicted
the rebirth of the nation—a nation was born again for a new

season in history. Circumcision marked the people's common identity and distinguished them from the nations of the world. It spoke of God's ownership and leadership of His people and their commonality of purpose.

The Israelites were circumcised with *"flint knives"*; that is, knives made from stone cut out from the mountain. Spiritually (and metaphorically), this could refer to the hand of God inscribing the divine principles into the hearts of His people. They were established to live a life that reflected the heavenly culture and an alternate manner of behaviour in a hostile and wicked world. The Prophet Jeremiah alluded to the circumcision of the heart and its application that went beyond a surgical procedure:

> *Circumcise yourselves to the Lord, and take away the foreskins of your hearts, you men of Judah and inhabitants of Jerusalem, lest My fury come forth like fire, and burn so that no one can quench it, because of the evil of your doings* (Jeremiah 4:4).

Circumcision: Enactment of an Ancient Principle

Here at Gilgal, an ancient spiritual principle was being enacted, thereby entrenching the covenant entered into by God and His people. According to Genesis, the rite of circumcision was a symbolic physical mark that signified the covenant entered into by God and Abraham, the founder and patriarchal father of the Israelites.[117] Through the covenant, a divine promise was entrenched, granting to Abraham and his seed the authority to inherit the land of Canaan, thereby qualifying the seed to be constituted as

---

[117] Genesis 17:1-14.

the "holy" nation of God.[118] It is in this respect that Abraham was instructed to "keep [Hebrew – *shamar*] the covenant" or "to tend and exercise great care over it", thereby preserving the significance of this sacred act in the life of the people.[119] Therefore circumcision was not only a physical act but also an emblematic way of reminding the Hebrew people of their responsibility to "pay careful attention to the obligations of the Covenant."[120] God expected the Hebrews to "keep" the requirements of the covenant, thus ensuring that it became an integral part of their lives.

Circumcision: Seal of Blessings

The seal of circumcision on Abraham affirmed the divine approval of a blameless life lived before God. It was also the assurance of the bestowal of blessings upon all future generations that followed his exemplary model. Righteous living was a prerequisite, permitting the right of entry into the divine privileges. Anything to the contrary invalidated this right of privilege. In the Epistle of Romans, prominence is placed on righteous living rather than on merely carrying a physical mark on one's body.[121] Abraham earned the reputation of being righteous long before he was circumcised. In so doing, he sent a clear message that circumspect and upright living is the seal of a circumcised life in the sight of God.

Does this blessedness then come upon the circumcised only, or upon the uncircumcised also? For we say that faith was accounted to Abraham for righteousness.

---

[118] Genesis 17:8.

[119] S. Zodhiates, ref. 8104, *shamar* means "to tend or exercise great care over it."

[120] S. Zodhiates, ref. 8104, p. 1671.

[121] Read Romans 4:9-12.

How then was it accounted? While he was circumcised,
or uncircumcised? Not while circumcised, but while
uncircumcised. And he received the sign of circumcision,
a seal of the righteousness of the faith which he had
while still uncircumcised, that he might be the father
of all those who believe, though they are uncircumcised,
that righteousness might be imputed to them also, and
the father of circumcision to those who not only are
of the circumcision, but who also walk in the steps of
the faith which our father Abraham had while still
uncircumcised (Romans 4:9-12).

It is notable that it was only after Abraham had circumcised himself (at the age of 99 years) and his entire male household that he received the angelic news of the imminent birth of Isaac, the son of promise.[122] A period of 24 years had already elapsed since Abraham had left Ur of the Chaldees in search of the promise, given to him by God.[123] Yet, it was only after he circumcised his household that he received the change of name from Abram to Abraham. From this it can be deduced that the rite of circumcision was an important factor in the activation of the promise of God. It is this fact that provokes the question, *Could it be that only after we publicly reflect a life totally surrendered to God, which bears the mark of divine ownership, that we will see the full activation of the promise(s) over our lives?* Our hearts must be circumcised, as it is here that God incubates His purpose, sets up His throne and establishes His sovereign rule.

---

[122] Genesis 18.

[123] Genesis 12.

Throughout the Old Testament, the rite of circumcision played a key role in the life of the Hebrew people. They could not advance into the purposes of God without maintaining the requirements of the covenant. The promise was preceded by a proviso that the nation of Israel would accept the dealings of God before they could be deemed capable of receiving the promise. It would seem that the rite of circumcision (and its spiritual application) is a foundational principle that determined whether one could access the divine favour and the fulfilment of the divine mandate. As we have noted, the rite of circumcision preceded the actual conquest of the land. Joshua was instructed by God to circumcise the nation at Gilgal before taking them into a military conquest of the land.

Even Moses was not exempted from enforcing the rite of circumcision on his family.

> *And it came to pass on the way, at the encampment, that the Lord met him and sought to kill him. Then Zipporah took a sharp stone and cut off the foreskin of her son and cast it at Moses' feet, and said, "Surely you are a husband of blood to me!" So He let him go. Then she said, "You are a husband of blood!"—because of the circumcision* (Exodus 4:24-26).

Moses had supernaturally received a clear mandate from God, at Mount Horeb, to return to Egypt and deliver the Hebrew people from slavery. While he and his family travelled to Egypt, God met with Moses and "attempted to kill him." Zipporah, the wife of Moses, intervened by circumcising her son, in response to the fearful encounter her husband had had with God. Her intervention halted the wrath of God and saved her husband from certain death. This was a bloody act that conveys a profound spiritual lesson: *One cannot legitimately respond and fulfil the divine mandate of a new season without ensuring that "his household" has observed and fulfilled the requirements of the rite of circumcision.* A divine calling on one's life, no matter how supernatural the encounter, cannot be fully activated unless that individual (and all those associated with the mandate of that individual) bears the seal of circumcision.

Circumcision: Sign of Divine Ownership

The rite of circumcision depicted divine ownership and a life totally consecrated to God. It became a "badge" that marked and distinguished the nation of Israel from the nations of the world and portrayed the covenant entered into between God and His people. By the removal of the foreskin, a message was transmitted to the world that the seed of Abraham are consecrated to God and that they are His community in the earth. The Israelites were severing or disconnecting themselves from any relations with Egypt or the systems of the world. It symbolizes the existence of a Holy Nation that receives its culture and constitution for living from a higher order—a way of life that will eventually overcome the systems of the world and establish the righteous Kingdom of God in the earth. This community adopted the divine constitution, which distinguished them from those who were not in covenant with God. They modelled to the nations a better way of living.

Realistically, the occupation of land was not the primary objective of the divine plan. There had to be a greater motivation. God wanted the Israelites to model a better way of living to all nations—a lifestyle conformed to the values of the heavens. Through the values of this Kingdom, He would subdue the earth and bring it back to godliness and peace. If the Israelites had merely been given land to satisfy their earthly desires, then it would be another futile exercise of gross divine injustice. *It is in this sense that I ponder on the purpose of any new season, if the advocates of that season do not reflect and introduce to the earth a higher and better standard of living.*

Circumcision: Love for God

Evidently, circumcision is more than just a physical mark. Moses associated circumcision with that of a life wholly dedicated to God:

> *And the Lord your God will circumcise your heart and the heart of your descendants, to love the Lord your God with all your heart and with all your soul, that you may live* (Deuteronomy 30:6).

Moses provided a spiritual application of circumcision with the sole purpose of bringing the people to a place of *loving* God with everything they had. The heart, which depicts the immaterial and inner nature of an individual, must be totally devoted to God. Circumcision, as a physical act, should reflect a passionate lifestyle of absolute love for God. Such "love" (Hebrew *ahab*), entails an "ardent and vehement inclination of the mind and a tenderness of affection at the same time."[124] An indictment against the Church at Ephesus was that they had departed from their first love.[125] Although Christ had forensically inspected this Church's works and found them commendable, He also rebuked them for having abandoned their love for Him. Their works were

---

[124] S. Zodhiates, ref. 157, p. 1708.

[125] Revelation 2:1ff.

not motivated by love but by an obsession for results. They were not depicting the fruit of a circumcised heart and were therefore found wanting.

> *But he is a Jew who is one inwardly; and circumcision is that of the heart, in the Spirit, not in the letter, whose praise is not from men but from God* (Romans 8:29).

The acknowledgment of a dedicated or circumcised life could not merely be elicited by popular opinion, but only by divine approval. Within the divine economy, the seal of circumcision on a congregation confirms the divine pleasure. There is absolutely no place for self-commendation or a feigned form of godliness. Only God can confer His approval. *In any new season, success must not be measured by one's accomplishments or apostolic works but by the quality and passion of one's love for God.*

Circumcision: Holy Living

I find it difficult to address the subject of circumcision without zeroing in on a holy and pure life lived in the presence of the Lord. Holiness is a way of life that simply cannot be relegated to insignificance in any new season of God. The Scriptures have laid out, in detail, the requirements for entry and active participation in the presence of God. Without preserving physical, moral and spiritual purity, it is impossible for the Church (in any move of God) to engage the holy presence.

The catastrophe that centred on Aaron's two sons, Nadab and Abihu, is a case in point. Their negligence in ensuring ceremonial protocol in approaching the presence of God resulted in their being consumed by a "strange fire." [126] They died before the Lord. Ungodliness violates the holiness of God and causes an outbreak of divine judgment. This is the reason for the insertion of the purity laws in the Old Testament. [127] These laws primarily instruct and guide people on the danger of approaching God in a manner that is inconsistent with His holy nature. The meticulous detail to structure (of the tabernacle and temple) and the strict adherence to procedure (by the priest in functioning within these structures) place emphasis on the holy nature of God.

Circumcision: The Rebirth of a Nation

Gilgal is the place where the nation was born again (for the second time). They had to stay at Gilgal until they were made "whole" (Hebrew *chayah*[128]). The meaning of this word *chayah* conveys the picture of the "birth of a nation," that is, of a nation being born or rebuilt. In this context, it can be said that circumcision depicted the death and resurrection of the nation that now lived under the supernatural power of God.

Arguably, a characteristic feature of changing seasons is the emergence of a new generation of people. This is the generation that was born in the "wilderness." However, they are required to be circumcised before they are capable of the responsibility and privileges that a new season heralds. There has to be the removal

---

[126] Refer to Numbers 9:15-23 and Leviticus 16:23 for examples of priestly protocols

[127] The Levitical laws on clean and unclean, purity and impurity were only detailed to the Israelites after the death of Nadab and Abihu. They were inserted to teach Israel that the manifest presence of God in their midst can only be sustained by clean living.

[128] S. Zodhiates. ref. 2421, *Chay*–In its literal senses, it means to "live again, to live, to enjoy life, to recover, to refresh, and to rebuild."

of the "old" if there is to be an embracing of the "new." This is the veil of flesh that prevents sight into the impending purposes of God for their generation. Their hearts must be configured and consecrated to God. This includes the recounting of the holy requirements that are a pre-condition for the literal possessing of the land. The royal law of God has to be clearly understood and adopted before they possess the promise.

The rite of circumcision is a bloody and painful procedure, and it also includes a period of healing. Gilgal is not only the place where people are circumcised, but also the place where people must be healed. *Church leaders must recognize that their people cannot effectively go further in their journey without those leaders first bringing them to the place of seriously confronting the heart-issues that plague their lives.* This is a time of diligent introspection, placing a demand on the renouncing of sin.

> *In Him you were also circumcised with the circumcision made without hands, by putting off the body of the sins of the flesh, by the circumcision of Christ, buried with Him in baptism, in which you also were raised with Him through faith in the working of God, who raised Him from the dead. And you, being dead in your trespasses and the uncircumcision of your flesh, He has made alive together with Him, having forgiven you all trespasses* (Colossians 2:11-13).

Church leaders must teach their people to ruthlessly overcome sin through *"the circumcision of Christ."* People are encouraged to exhibit the character of Christ in every facet of their lives.

> *And have put on the new man, which is renewed in*
> *knowledge after the image of him that created him:*
> *where there is neither Greek nor Jew, circumcision*
> *nor uncircumcision, Barbarian, Scythian, bond nor*
> *free: but Christ is all, and in all. Put on therefore, as*
> *the elect of God, holy and beloved, bowels of mercies,*
> *kindness, humbleness of mind, meekness, longsuffering;*
> *forbearing one another, and forgiving one another, if*
> *any man have a quarrel against any: even as Christ*
> *forgave you, so also do ye. And above all these things put*
> *on charity, which is the bond of perfectness. And let the*
> *peace of God rule in your hearts, to the which also ye*
> *are called in one body; and be ye thankful. Let the word*
> *of Christ dwell in you richly in all wisdom; teaching*
> *and admonishing one another in psalms and hymns*
> *and spiritual songs, singing with grace in your hearts to*
> *the Lord. And whatsoever ye do in word or deed, do all*
> *in the name of the Lord Jesus, giving thanks to God and*
> *the Father by him* (Colossians 3:10-17 KJV).

Paul contributes a great deal to our understanding and application of the significance and the role of circumcision in the New Covenant. According to Paul, the physical rite of circumcision does not make the Jews legitimate members of God's family.

> *For he is not a Jew, which is one outwardly; neither*
> *is that circumcision, which is outward in the flesh*
> (Romans 2:28 KJV).

For Paul, circumcision is an inward mark revealing a devout life lived before God. It is a life of separation from the worldly culture. A person is not a Christian or a Jew by an outward mark but by an inward life walked blamelessly before God. As stated earlier, the seal of circumcision on Abraham was the sign of a blameless life lived and walked before God.

In any given season, there must be an entire generation of believers who espouse the covenant of God by a demonstration of circumspect living. Church leaders cannot engage the divine mandate or publicly proclaim the message of a new season before ensuring that it is modelled in their congregations and ministries.

It is in this regard that Paul viewed circumcision as the spiritual mark that characterized and distinguished the community of God from the rest of the world. Paul teaches that the depth and quality of the believer's lifestyle validates and legitimises one's claim to membership in the family of God.[129] He asserts that one's membership is not determined by observance of a ritualistic procedure, but by a life depicting the new birth.

> *For in Christ Jesus neither circumcision nor uncircumcision avails anything, **but a new creation*** [my emphasis] (Galatians 6:15).

Circumcision: Validates the Message Preached

Our justification as servants of God is found in the example we live before those who judge us. The evidence of a circumcised life is *seen* by the quality of a life lived before God and people. There has to be a visible manifestation of a community that captures and reflects a dynamic lifestyle, a lifestyle that is compliant with the message proclaimed by that community. The marks of circumcision are reflected in an exemplary lifestyle that is in total

---

[129] Galatians 6:15.

harmony with the divine law. A circumspect life exonerates the Law of God in the eyes of the sceptic and at the same time exempts the believer from being judged by the same law. Compatibility between the message preached and the messenger preaching is a fundamental prerequisite for any form of witnessing.

A valuable lesson from Gilgal is that leaders of the Church must build and create communities based on quality and not merely on quantity. People are not simply called Christian by accepting Christ into their lives but by demonstrating the lifestyle of Christ in the earth. The seal of circumcision is the bestowal of God's favour upon the believer based upon a life that portrays the message of Christ to the earth. In other words, *there cannot be the proclamation of the message until it has been incarnated into the life of the believer individually and the congregation corporately.* The "Word must become flesh and dwell among us."[130] When the congregation becomes a "model"[131] of the message, then the nations are attracted to those who are heralds of it.

> *What advantage then has the Jew, or what is the profit of circumcision? Much in every way! Chiefly because to them were committed the oracles of God. For what if some did not believe? Will their unbelief make the faithfulness of God without effect? Certainly not! Indeed, let God be true but every man a liar. As it is written:* ***"That You may be justified in Your words, and may overcome when You are judged"*** [my emphasis] (Romans 3:1-4).

---

[130] John 1:14.

[131] S. Zodhiates, ref. 5179, *tupos,* a type, example or model–a constituent element of that which is yet to appear.

In the New Testament, the rite of circumcision is translated into the context of the Christian experience. It was also one of the leading controversies that almost divided the entire Church. At the first Apostolic Council of the early Church, the matter was resolved, and this brought definition to the Church's understanding regarding circumcision.[132] Here it was accepted that, in Christ, there was no wall of demarcation between Jew and Gentile, since God had cleansed (Greek *katharsis*) their hearts by faith. It sounded out the message that there was no discrimination in Christ. There was neither circumcised nor uncircumcised— everyone who received Christ into his or her life was unified by Him and enjoyed the same benefits.

Circumcision and the Apostolic Reformation

The Apostolic Reformation is motivated by the desire to see a "perfect man" patterned in the image of Jesus Christ in the earth. This "man" is a corporate man; that is, it is the Body of Christ. The principal message of circumcision in the New Testament communicates the idea of "making" through the blood of Jesus Christ *"one new man."* [133] The believers are no longer alienated from God but are *"fellow citizens with the saints and members of the household of God."*[134]

The message of circumcision destroys the walls of demarcation and creates a new identity for the believer. It is a sign of the complex and indivisible nature divinely intended for the Body of Christ. The circumcised, irrespective of race or colour, are members of the household of God. They are a pivotal part of a new

---

[132] Acts 15:9-11.

[133] Ephesians 2:11-22.

[134] Ephesians 2:19.

nation in the earth. Therefore, every form of division must be confronted and radically eliminated from the Church of Jesus Christ.

Leaders should make every effort to build the value system of God in each member of their congregations. Hearts have to be configured to live out the righteous requirements of the heavenly order. Hence, there is the call to "circumcise the heart or to remove the foreskin of the heart."[135] The flint knives cut out of the Rock are the surgical instruments used to circumcise the heart. This "stony" instrument is the *principle(s)* cut out from the eternal Word (the Logos), which is the Rock of our salvation. These divine principles are "hid" or installed in the heart of the believers so that their lives are regulated to serve the Lord and not to sin against Him. It is therefore imperative to remember that a holistic lifestyle in compliance with the divine requirements is the manifest fruit of a circumcised heart:

> *And the Lord your God will circumcise your heart and the heart of your descendants, to love the Lord your God with all your heart and with all your soul, that you may live* (Deuteronomy 30:6).

Leaders cannot take their people forward into God's purpose without implementing a "programme of circumcision." This is the removal of the abstract from the concrete. The circumcised are those who have received the approval of God. The validation of the believer's life elevates the believer to the place of becoming the oracle of God in the earth.[136] These believers have been

---

[135] Jeremiah 4:4.

[136] Romans 3:1-25.

accredited with the privilege of declaring the Word of God. Without a circumspect lifestyle, the carrier of the message will not be justified in the eyes of the beholder.[137] The message of God is judged by the circumspect lifestyle of the messengers. Even Jesus was a *diakonos* (minister) of the circumcision for the truth of God, to confirm the promise made to the fathers.[138]

> *Now I say that Jesus Christ has become a servant to the circumcision for the truth of God, to confirm the promises made to the fathers* (Romans 15:8).

The strength of the divine promise was determined by the presentation of a life that certified the pledge made by God. Paul challenged the behaviour of Peter who perjured his relationship with the "uncircumcised" Gentile Christians in the presence of his "circumcised" Jewish counterparts.[139] Paul's point of contention was based on the biblical fact that if the messenger of God violates the spirit and message of Christ, it then relegates Christ to being classified as *"a minister of sin."*[140] *A Church that preaches a message without visibly demonstrating it in an accurate lifestyle is a counterfeit.* The authenticity of the believer constituted a truly apostolic Church.

> *Knowing that a man is not justified by the works of the law but by faith in Jesus Christ, even we have believed in Christ Jesus, that we might be justified by faith in*

---

[137] Romans 3:4.

[138] Romans 15:8.

[139] Galatians 2:11-16.

[140] Galatians 2:17.

> *Christ and not by the works of the law; for by the works*
> *of the law no flesh shall be justified. But if, while we*
> *seek to be justified by Christ, we ourselves also are found*
> *sinners, is Christ therefore a minister of sin? Certainly*
> *not!* (Galatians 2:16-17) .

In the Epistle to the Philippians, Paul warns against "false circumcision"[141:]

> *For we are the circumcision, who worship God in the*
> *Spirit, rejoice in Christ Jesus, and have no confidence in*
> *the flesh* (Philippians 3:3).

Observing the commandments of God is a critical prerequisite to pleasing God in the ministry of the Church.[142] Clearly, obedience to the Word of God is placed higher than a physical outward sign or mark.

> *Circumcision is nothing, and uncircumcision is*
> *nothing, but the keeping of the commandments of God*
> (1 Corinthians. 7:19).

This season asks the searching question, 'Is it possible to have come out of Egypt but still have the veil of Egypt over the heart?' Against this backdrop, circumcision may be defined as that painful process of forcefully confronting and dealing with the issues of the heart and the internal life of every true believer of Christ, so that out of an inward life lived, Christ can be clearly revealed

---

[141] Philippians 3:3.

[142] 1 Corinthians 7:19.

to the earth. This is an agonizing process and the veil of flesh can only be removed by the flint knife of God's holy laws or divine principles.

In the Apostolic Reformation, the message of circumcision calls for the revisiting of the principles of the Abrahamic Covenant, where the preconditions for triumphant and successful living are clearly outlined. By dealing with the issues of the heart and the organisation of the inward man, a message could be sent into the world of a life totally dedicated and owned by God. The hallmark of an apostolic people is founded on a lifestyle of total surrender to God.

The message of the Apostolic Reformation calls for the conquest of every hostile system of government that stands in opposition to the will of God for the earth. The apostolic anointing is released to eradicate the forces of darkness and establish a kingdom of light. However, this cannot be accomplished by a people who are no different in character and behaviour to the world. Every believer who seeks to be an integral part of the end-time purposes of God must carry, on themselves, the badge of circumcision. In this way they are declaring allegiance and ownership to God. By forcefully removing the foreskin of the flesh from their lives and demonstrating it through a living faith in God, they are making a declaration to the world that they have committed their lives totally to God. The removal of the foreskin from their "hearts" depicts a holistic life lived completely for God.

CHAPTER 6

The Feast of Passover

Now the children of Israel camped in Gilgal, and kept
the Passover on the fourteenth day of the month at
twilight on the plains of Jericho (Joshua 5:10).

The Israelites celebrated the Passover at Gilgal on the four-teenth day of the first month of the new year. Joshua was cel-ebrating an everlasting covenant entered into by his ancestor, Abraham. In so doing, he highlighted the significant place that the Feast of Passover occupied in the life of every Israelite.

The Passover served as a beacon directing the nation of Israel to an ancient landmark. It also helped them to recount and retell the story of their journey through the past to their present posi-tion. Identification with the process of the past helped them to bring validation, affirmation and strength to their present reality. This, in turn, encouraged them to be totally committed to the God of their destiny.

The partaking of the first Passover meal was conducted with the idea of a whole nation being prepared for deliverance from Egypt, the house of slavery. The Hebrews partook of their meal standing, dressed for a hasty departure away from an oppressive system of governance.[143]

> *…Belt on your waist, your sandals on your feet, and your staff in your hand…* (Exodus 12:11).

This was a journey to liberty. It was their night of freedom. It was an assurance of immunity as they entered into a hostile environment and the uncertainties of a new season. According to Hebrews, the Passover and the sprinkling of the blood provided the protective hedge that preserved the Israelites from the power of death.[144] It is evident that the Israelites would not enjoy unconditional immunity from the power of death until they brought themselves under the covering of the blood of the slain lamb. The observance of the Feast was an act of faith that clearly demonstrated the belief that God would protect and preserve His people from the evil that was in the land. It guaranteed the safety of the people in the journey toward destiny.

The meal characterized the night of *"solemn observance,"* a very serious time in the existence of the people.[145] Their safety lay in the observance of the divine instructions. Eating the meal was fundamental to the success of their travel from the house of slavery to the house of freedom. A divine judgment was coming into the land, and only those who had the blood of the sacrificed animal were exempt.[146] There could be no place for complacency or a false sense of security. This was a war against the spirits of the

---

[143] Exodus 12:14,17,24,,42.

[144] Hebrews 11:28.

[145] Exodus 12:42.

[146] Exodus 12:13.

land, when the principality over Egypt would be dealt the final blow.[147] The time (twilight) of the sacrifice of the Passover is the point of the deliverance of Israel from Egypt's bondage.[148] At the point of the sacrifice of the animals, their deliverance was in effect completed despite the fact that the final deathblow was only dealt against the god(s) of Egypt at midnight.

> *But at the place where the Lord your God chooses*
> *to make His name abide, there you shall sacrifice the*
> *Passover at twilight, at the going down of the sun,*
> ***at the time you came out of Egypt*** [my emphasis]
> (Deuteronomy 16:6).

The first Passover marked the day of deliverance from the wicked system of Egypt. The Hebrew word *pesah,* for Passover, means "God leaped or passed over" the houses of Israel when He brought judgment against the Egyptians.[149] Every other Passover is actually a *celebration* of that great day of deliverance and all the benefits that it provided for every other generation of Israelites— to live triumphantly over the wicked forces of darkness.

One of the requirements of the Passover feast was that the whole lamb had to be eaten[150]—there was to be no wastage or leftovers. This symbolically stresses the need for the sharing of the entire sacrificial lamb. It is a pictorial depiction of the signif-

---

[147] Exodus 12:12.

[148] Deuteronomy 16:6.

[149] S. Zodhiates, ref. 6452; Exodus 12:13,23,27.

[150] According to the requirements, there were certain parts of the Passover lamb that had to be burnt since they were not edible. The lesson being communicated by this point is that the whole lamb was sacrificed for the deliverance of the nation.

icance of the sacrifice. To partake of the whole sacrificial lamb is to ensure preservation from the judgment of death or to have the assurance to life. To participate in the Passover is to partake of life.[151] In the New Covenant, Christ, the ultimate Passover lamb, promised eternal life to all who partook of Him. *"Then Jesus said to them, 'Most assuredly, I say to you, unless you eat the flesh of the Son of Man and drink His blood, you have no life in you.'"[152]*

The spirit of Reformation is like a fine tuning fork. It seeks to adjust and realign the Church to the salient principle(s) of divine function. This season in God must therefore be interpreted through the lessons gleaned from the Feast of Passover. If the Church is to accurately enter into this new season, then it must circumspectly apply the significant lesson and principles of the Passover to its current processes.

Passover: Initiator of New Beginnings

In the Old Covenant, the Feast of Passover did not only mark the beginning of a new year, but it also brought closure to the previous season before a new door was opened. It was celebrated on the fourteenth day of the first month of the year in the calendar of the Israelites. Allow me to take the liberty of asserting that it typified the activation of new beginnings or new initiatives in the unfolding plans of God and that it introduced the celebration of newness. In this regard, any new season in God must make the Passover the critical point of departure, with the assurance that by the observation of all that it represents one finds the Church's greatest victories.

---

[151] John 6:51-58,

[152] John 6:53,

The Church must bring back the Passover to its exact place in the Body of Christ. In the New Covenant, the principles of the Passover and their application are fundamental to successful Christian living. *Christ is the Passover Lamb of the Church.*[153] The Feast of Passover details, for the believer, the magnitude of our deliverance and the extent of God's love for His people in that He gave us such a perfect sacrifice.

In every Reformation there has been a revisiting of the ordinance of the Passover Feast and the restoration of its purpose to the appropriate place in the Body of Christ. With the reinterpretation of the central role that the Passover plays in the life and works of the Church, there emerges the need to judge everything within the scope of the Church's practice. All ritualistic and legalistic practice that emphasise the works of people must be eradicated. The entire Church must be established on a clear understanding related to the principle of divine grace.

Passover: Didactic Element

Those who embrace the necessity of an Apostolic Reformation of the Church must make the Passover *a central aspect of their teachings*. At every Passover celebration there was a recital of the story of the redemption from Egypt. This was the time when the Israelites revisited the story of their deliverance and made it alive to their children. In this way they reconciled the workings of God in His relationship with them as a nation. Each Jewish male had to recite the story to his children so that they could identify with their supernatural existence and ascribe deliverance to the sovereign workings of God. As a result, every generation

---

[153] 1 Corinthians 5:7-8.

could remember the day of their salvation and credit God with the reasons for their success in life's journey.

In my opinion, the didactic element of redemption has been neglected in the Christian home and Church. Consequently, many people (including our children) in the Church of Jesus Christ do not fully understand the extent of the message of the salvation of the human race. For this reason, there is gross disregard for so great a salvation.

There cannot be more emphasis on the fact that every benefit a believer enjoys is directly associated with Christ Jesus, our Passover. Unless the message of redemption is etched in the mind of the believer, he or she will not be able to fully enjoy and appreciate his or her deliverance from the wicked snare of the evil one. By bringing back a fresh emphasis on the meritorious work of our redemption, we make the choice of developing a "Christocentric" (Christ-centred) gospel that removes the fleshly works of humans from the centre stage of the sovereign acts of God.

Those in the Apostolic Reformation have got to make Christ, the Passover Lamb, the compass for the journey. When leaders reflect on the day of humankind's deliverance in Christ, they recount, retell and identify with salvation. In this course of action, alignment and affirmation is brought to the present, thereby making a commitment to the future. By such proclamation, the faith of the believer is informed, encouraged and developed. It then becomes a subjective reality that God's people are immunised against the perils of the journey ahead of them.

The Cross

In the New Covenant, the Passover finds its fullest expression and meaning in the spiritual symbolism of the Cross. The Cross is the symbol of the great victory Christ had accomplished for the

Church, when He had destroyed the forces of evil and emancipated humanity.

The Cross is the crux of the New Covenant. It is the pivotal point through which everything in the Christian faith is processed, interpreted and activated. Without the Cross, the Christian faith is reduced to a place of mere religion. There is absolutely no entry into the presence of the Lord outside of the Cross. Whenever the Church moves away from the Cross, the central point of her existence, the Church arrives at a place of crisis in history.

In every Reformation there has been a clarion call to return to the point of departure. One of the watermarks of Martin Luther's Reformation was the re-emphasis on the meritorious work of Christ on the Cross of Calvary and the call for the Church of his day to redefine the means of salvation to the sinner. Hence the restoration of the truth *"the just shall live by faith"* and that the sinner is saved by "grace through faith in Christ Jesus."[154] The Cross of Jesus Christ, the Passover Lamb, abolishes the Law and introduces the believer to the period of grace. It reminds humanity that there is no salvation without partaking of the whole lamb. Christ, and Christ alone, sufficiently provides salvation and access into the community of God. Thus, the Passover is not only central to all religious activity but is also the foundation of all Christian activity.

History teaches us that in every reformation there was an interpretation or reinterpretation of the spiritual significance of the Passover Feast. The reformers, like King Josiah (in the Old Testament) and Luther, reintroduced the importance of the Passover to the life and function of God's people. Its application was brought to bear on the whole operation of the Church.

---

[154] Hebrews 10:38; Ephesians 2:8.

For example, in the Reformation of King Josiah, there was a restoration of the spiritual significance and redefinition of the Feast of Passover.[155] He restructured the priesthood, restoring them to their divinely ordained ministry functions. He also reorganised the worship ministry and positioned the gatekeepers in their correct places. He did this to ensure that the spiritual climate was correct for the celebration of the Feast of the Passover. The Passover was brought back to its appointed place. Therefore, he received the acclamation of celebrating a Passover that was "never like anything since the days of Samuel."[156]

Passover: Salvation by Grace

"Salvation by grace through faith in Christ" is one of the most salient interpretations that the spirit of true reformation brings to the Church. It asserts that the works of people is not the medium for accessing the favour of God. Access to God is through Christ, the Passover Lamb. The earthly works or ability of people cannot justifiably stand in the presence of God. It is only through the works of Christ that the divine approval is granted.

This point is best illustrated in the story of Cain and Abel.[157] The name Cain means "I have begotten, created or procured a man."[158] He is the epitome of a self-made man who is driven by personal ideals for success. His parents gave birth to him probably with the hope that he would be the seed of a man who would bruise the head of the serpent.[159] Upon him lay the hope of fallen

---

[155] 2 Chronicles 35:1-19; 2 Kings 23:21; Ezra 6:19.

[156] 2 Kings 23:21-23.

[157] Genesis 4:1ff.

[158] S. Zodhiates, ref. 7014.

[159] Genesis 3:15.

humanity. He typifies the caricature of a humanistic ideology that "man" is intrinsically good, that he is in control of his own fate and that he can determine his own destiny. It is this ideology that produces a "cultural Christianity" that is a synchronisation of humanistic ideals and biblical values. It invalidates the power of the Cross and cancels the sacrificial work Christ accomplished for the entire human race.

On the contrary, the name Abel means "I am nothing, vain, empty, and unsatisfactory."[160] Abel conveys the idea of being "vain in action, word, or expectation." In other words, he represents that type of individual who has died to self and has permitted the efficacious ministry of God to work through him. He is a representative of pure religion. In him is found the embodiment of biblical Christianity where one's entire life is governed by the eternal values of God and not by one's own assessment of life. He typifies salvation by grace through faith in God.

The Church of our time has neglected many aspects of the significance of the Passover. The Passover, symbolised by the Cross, has been reduced to a mere symbol of religious importance. The Table is relegated to a place of ritualistic observance. Sadly, a segment of the Church is guilty of imposing the sentence of death upon itself. The place of salvation has become the object of sacrilegious and ignorant worship. It has gone back to an emphasis on salvation by works. Heavy burdens are placed on its adherents. This is the reason for its decay and weak state of existence. A large percentage of the "church" is living according to the law of works. The structure(s) of the Church is reeking with the smell of human perspiration. Its activity is measured by the estimate of human works. These works include the prayer programmes,

---

[160] S. Zodhiates, ref. 1893.

forms of liturgy, acts of charity, systems and functions of government. The motivation behind these works is the impure desire
for selfish gain and self aggrandisement. The contemporary culture of the "church" is designed to encourage human endeavours,
egotistical desires and humanistic ideals. They replace the values and lessons that the Feast of Passover communicates to the
Church. Therefore it is imperative that leaders of congregations
seriously revisit the principles derived from the Feasts of Passover
and make the necessary adjustments. The Table of the Lord can
become that place of evaluation.

Table of Communion

The Table of the Lord is significant in the liturgy of the Church.
The celebration of the Table of the Lord provides an appropriate
place for critical evaluation as regards to the centrality of Christ
(and all that He represents) in the Church, both individually and
corporately. Although this is the place to remember the Lord, it
is also at this place that the searching voice of the Lord must be
heard: *"Someone will betray Me."*

The Table presents the opportunity for self-analysis. It is the
period of purifying and cleaning out anything that was unleavened. The leaven is the bread of affliction—the diet of Egypt that
brought great sorrow to Israel.[161] Any negative influence that
draws the believer away from Christ must be eliminated. Christ
refers to this as the leaven of the Pharisees and Sadducees.[162]
Through the process of self-examination, *"Let a man examine
himself,"* it can be ascertained where exactly an individual is in his

---

[161] Deuteronomy 16:3-4.

[162] Matthew 16:6.

or her relationship with Christ.[163] The examination takes place at the "Table." The diet of the Passover is the body of Christ and His blood.[164] By partaking of Christ, the unleavened bread—the "unleavened bread of sincerity and truth"—the contaminating elements of the world are removed from the life of a believer. There can be no movement forward into the unfolding purpose of God without the Church coming back to the Cross of "sincerity and truth." At the Cross, the believer must die to self, and by partaking of the elements at the Table, there is the celebration of personal purity.

This was the offering where the whole lamb was to be eaten by every Hebrew household that wanted deliverance and protection from the imminent judgment that was to be imposed on Egypt. The whole Hebrew nation was in bondage to Pharaoh and needed to be collectively liberated. By eating of the Passover, they were declaring their separation from a hostile system of governance that enslaved and restricted them. Even the detailed symbolism of the meal clearly communicates this fact:

> *You shall eat no leavened bread with it; seven days you shall eat unleavened bread with it, that is, the bread of affliction (for you came out of the land of Egypt in haste), that you may remember the day in which you came out of the land of Egypt all the days of your life* (Deuteronomy 16:3).

---

[163] 1 Corinthians 11:28. (Read 1 Peter 2:24; Matthew 26:17-30; Mark 14; Luke 9:51.)

[164] Matthew 26:26-29.

The bitter herbs denoted the bitterness of their slavery and the necessity of separation from all corruption. By partaking of it, they were stating their conscious choice of changing their diet from anything that corrupts, pollutes or enslaves. It placed a demand for separation from the worldly way of life. This meal would remind them to refrain from any form of fellowship that permits influential elements to corrupt their way.[165]

> *Therefore purge out the old leaven, that you may be a new lump, since you truly are unleavened. For indeed Christ, our Passover, was sacrificed for us. Therefore let us keep the feast, not with old leaven, nor with the leaven of malice and wickedness, but with the unleavened bread of sincerity and truth* (1 Corinthians 5:7-8).

Passover: The Blood

There are two very clear aspects to the Passover. One is the preparation and eating of the Passover lamb. The other is the sprinkling of the blood on the doorpost and lintels of each house-hold of the Israelites. The Passover is like a spiritual generator that releases the power for God's purpose to be fulfilled in the new season—the blood releasing the supernatural power for divine accomplishments. The blood marks the believers and preserves them from the rest of humanity. It was the celebration of immu-nity. You are preserved from the prevailing judgment. The Passo-ver and the sprinkling of the blood released faith, in that God will preserve the Hebrew people from the power of death.[166] Deviation

---

[165] Matthew 16:6.

[166] Read Hebrew 11:28.

from the principles of Passover opened the door for the breaching of divine immunity from the hostile forces in our world.

Passover highlights the significance of the blood; *the "ordinance" of the blood is an everlasting one.*[167] In it lies the expiatory principle: an animal was killed so that another life, under judgment, was spared. The beneficiaries were redeemed by blood not only from judgment but to be God's own possession. While sin exposes people's nakedness, the blood atones or covers their sins and reconciles them to God. The blood provides the divine "cover-up" through which sin is cancelled and reconciliation may then take place between fallen humanity and God. At the Cross, sin was dealt with by the shed blood of Jesus Christ.

> *Who Himself bore our sins in His own body on the tree, that we, having died to sins, might live for righteousness—by whose stripes you were healed* (1 Peter 2:24).

The Feast of Passover was the celebration of posterity preservation. Through this demonstration of faith, a profound statement was made that God will protect His people from the evil in the land. It was the celebration of community and covenant. *What I have becomes yours.* By celebrating the Passover, the Israelites were sharing in a communal bond that demonstrated their relation to each other and to the family of heaven. This unity was made possible through the Passover lamb that was sacrificed.

One of the most notable Passover feasts observed in the Old Testament (since the days of Solomon) was that of Hezekiah.[168] It

---

[167] Exodus 12:24-25; 13:10.

[168] Read 2 Chronicles 30.

was celebrated in the second month, only after the consecration of the backslidden priesthood and the gathering of the people at Jerusalem. Hezekiah ensured that it was kept in the *"prescribed"* way, since it had not been done for a long time. From Jerusalem, he sent out a call to the 12 tribes to repent of their sinful and errant ways and come together to celebrate the Passover. Many mocked him and rejected the invitation, but there were many who responded with *"singleness of heart"* and came to Jerusalem. Here, they destroyed the false altars with the priests expressing shame for their inaccurate lifestyle and practices. The results were far reaching in that those who were not sanctified received sanctification and many were healed. This released the spirit of true worship and singing, with people giving generous freewill peace offerings and the prayers of the Levites entering into the heavens and being heard. So great was the experience that they extended the celebration for a further 14 days.

I cannot refrain from posing these questions: Is it possible that the present sickly state of the Church is directly related to its lack of understanding and true celebration of the Passover? Could it be possible that this present Reformation can help reestablish the true value of the Table of the Lord and thereby create the spiritual atmosphere for a restoration of the presence of the Lord in His Church? It will be a great joy to receive the commendation of the heavens that, after such a long time, the Table of the Lord has been celebrated in His Church with spiritual propriety.

CHAPTER 7

The Change of Economic Policy

And they ate of the produce of the land on the day after the Passover, unleavened bread and parched grain, on the very same day. Then the manna ceased on the day after they had eaten the produce of the land; and the children of Israel no longer had manna, but they ate the food of the land of Canaan that year
(Joshua 5:11-12).

Gilgal set the stage for the *economic* transformation of the Israelite nation. Here, the Israelites were transitioned from being a society of subservient consumers to that of becoming producers. After 40 years of wandering in the wilderness, the daily heavenly diet of manna abruptly ended, signifying a change in the economic and social state of the nation. The people had to migrate from a place of passive dependence on the miraculous provision of manna to a place of aggressively and independently working the land.

This does not imply that they no longer needed to depend on God as the source of their daily needs. The long-awaited day had dawned when they would not only possess the land but also enjoy their inheritance as individuals as well as a nation. After centuries of being landless, they emerged to a situation of empowerment. Consequently, the quality of their lives would be immeasurably improved. The termination of manna sent a powerful message: *They must live off the land*. God wanted His people to partake of and enjoy the many blessings from the land that He had promised to their fathers—a land flowing with "milk and honey."

Since the diet of the nation had changed, new strategies had to be adopted together with the implementation of a sustainable plan of action that would guarantee their well-being in a hostile environment. Theirs was an amazing accelerated transition. In the same year that they crossed over the Jordan, they partook of their first harvest of the land.

Joshua: Economic Mantle of Anointing

A careful study of Joshua's leadership brings me to the conclusion that the divine *purpose* of a given season determines the choice of leader and the grace required for the fulfilment of the tasks in that season. Hence, it is my view that Joshua's appointment was not primarily motivated by the fact that he was a faithful servant or prodigy of Moses, or that he was one of the two spies who reconnoitred the land and returned with a positive report. Although these are plausible motivations, the choice was governed by a greater reason.[169] I am of the opinion that the principal mantle of grace upon Joshua's life was an economic anointing. Joshua was handpicked because he possessed the ability to

---

[169] Deuteronomy 31:7.

facilitate the dynamic process of economic empowerment. In essence, Joshua's mandate was to lead the nation across the River Jordan and bring them into their inheritance. His responsibilities included the military process of systematically possessing the land and distributing the inheritances to the people.

The appointment of Joshua was also accentuated by the fact that he was the leader of the tribe of Ephraim.[170] Permit me to explain. By establishing Joshua as leader over Israel, God was honouring the principle of the *firstborn*. When one traces the lineage of Joshua, one discovers that he is a descendent of Ephraim, whose father was Joseph. Joseph was the firstborn son of Jacob, the result of a patriarchal promise passed on to him because of the default of Reuben, Jacob's biological firstborn. Reuben, the firstborn son of Leah, abdicated his firstborn status when he had a sexual relationship with his father's concubine.[171] The consequence of Reuben's transgression was the removal of his executive privilege as the firstborn; a privilege that was then conferred on Joseph, who was the eleventh son of Jacob but the first by his second wife Rachel.

There may be many mitigating reasons for the installation of Joshua as leader of the Israelite nation.

Firstly, divine protocol was firmly established when Joshua was appointed as leader over the Israelites. The patriarchal blessing was associated with the privilege of the *firstborn*. God was acknowledging and respecting a fundamental patriarchal promise that was entered into between Jacob and Joseph. This involved the prophecy of Jacob over Ephraim, Joseph's second son. According

---

[170] Numbers 13:8.

[171] 1 Chronicles 5:1.

to Genesis,[172] Jacob adopted Joseph's two sons (Jacob's grandsons), Manasseh and Ephraim, and elevated them to a position of significance and legitimacy among the tribes of Israel.

When Jacob blessed his grandsons, he placed Ephraim, the second son, above Manasseh, the eldest son. By "skilfully" placing his right hand on the head of Ephraim, he enforced a change in the chronological order of the genealogy of his grandsons.[173] The younger son was elevated to the position of the *firstborn* and consequently received the responsibility of fulfilling the functions and enjoying the privileges of the firstborn, which included a double portion of the inheritance.

It is in this context that it makes sense that a son of Ephraim enjoys the privilege of leading God's people across the Jordan into the Promised Land. Joshua, being the leader of the tribe of Ephraim, had the privilege, as the leader of the *firstborn* tribe, to lead the rest of the tribes into the Promised Land and to expedite the process of dividing and distributing the land to the people.[174]

Secondly, the principal grace upon Joshua is found in understanding the principal grace of the tribe of Ephraim.[175] Ephraim is the second son of Joseph, born in Egypt of Asenath, the daughter of Poti-Pherah, the priest of On.[176] The name *Ephraim* means "double fruitful in the land of affliction."[177] The name is associated with prosperity, inheritance and possessing the land. Ephraim

---

[172] Genesis 48.

[173] Genesis 48:18.

[174] Numbers 13:8.

[175] Read Genesis 41:52.

[176] Genesis 41:50-52.

[177] S. Zodhiates, ref. 6509; Genesis 41:52.

was born during the seven years of plenty, so his boyhood years overlapped with the last 17 years of life of his grandfather Jacob, who had migrated to Egypt during the years of famine. By naming him Ephraim, Joseph was acknowledging that this child was a sign and seal of the abundant blessings of God in an alien land of great affliction. Hence, Ephraim became a symbol of prosperity and affluent living. It is also interesting to note that Joseph had a tremendous grace in the world of economics. He introduced the most ingenious economic reforms to the land of Egypt. It was the economic programs that Joseph implemented that made Egypt a powerful nation in the world during a time of great famine. Joseph's divinely inspired programme of food aid for the people of the world not only brought economic salvation to the global community, it also made Pharaoh one of the most powerful feudal lords in the world.

In this regard, Ephraim became the symbol of the fruitfulness and prosperity that highlighted the phenomenal rise to power and prosperity Joseph enjoyed in Egypt. Pharaoh named him Zaphnath–Paaneah, meaning "God speaks and lives through you."[178] He recognised that God had given Joseph insight into the future that would help preserve life. Undoubtedly, God did speak and preserve life through Joseph. This is highlighted by Joseph's words to his brothers: *"God sent me before you to preserve a posterity for you in the earth, and to save your lives by a great deliverance."*[179] Joseph was sent to preserve the world as well as God's chosen people. If they had not survived this difficult time in history, there would have been no salvation and blessing for the nations. It is in this respect that salvation and preservation came in the form

---

[178] Genesis 41:45.

[179] Genesis 45:7; read also Genesis 50:20.

of economic blessings. Even the prophecy over Joseph's life lends support to this assumption that his greatest strengths were in the world of economics.

Jacob, before departing from the earth, prophesied that Joseph will be very prosperous.

> *Joseph is a fruitful bough, a fruitful bough by a well;*
> *his branches run over the wall. The archers have bitterly*
> *grieved him, shot at him and hated him. But his bow*
> *remained in strength, and the arms of his hands were*
> *made strong by the hands of the Mighty God of Jacob*
> *from there is the Shepherd, the Stone of Israel), by*
> *the God of your father who will help you, and by the*
> *Almighty who will bless you with blessings of heaven*
> *above, blessings of the deep that lies beneath, blessings*
> *of the breasts and of the womb. The blessings of your*
> *father have excelled the blessings of my ancestors, up to*
> *the utmost bound of the everlasting hills. They shall be*
> *on the head of Joseph, and on the crown of the head*
> *of him who was separate from his brothers* (Genesis
> 49:22-26).

What needs to be highlighted is that Joseph was a tremendously anointed person who was totally committed and dependent on his God. His life reflects his competence, the high moral values he espoused (evidenced in his response to Potiphar's wife) and his total dependence upon God for the interpretation of his dreams and visions.[180]

---

180 Genesis 41:16.

Thirdly, God appointed Joshua as leader over the nation so that he would bring economic salvation to the people. Economic salvation is an integral part of the heart of God for His people and should not be treated as a carnal and unspiritual aspect of life. Under Joshua's leadership, the people were transitioned into a community of landowners with an enterprising spirit. This does not, in any way, infer that Joshua will be lesser in his commitment to a devout and holy lifestyle, or that he will discredit the teachings of Moses. It must be borne in mind that he was mentored by Moses himself and that he personally enjoyed the presence of God in the mountain and tabernacle.[181] Therefore, as Moses' servant (Hebrew *sharath*[182]), Joshua was probably an embodiment of everything that his master had taught him. He was fully associated with the life, works and teachings of his mentor.. Although he would continue to walk in the footsteps of Moses, God would elevate Joshua to a level where he would be imbued with the exact grace to successfully lead His people through this leg of the journey. This does not necessarily negate the emphasis of the last season to a place of insignificance. All that Moses had taught Joshua was still relevant, even though the assignment and the characteristic features of the new season were different.

Joshua: The Conquest of Canaan

His 30 years of leadership primarily focussed on "the conquest of the land." The programme of conquest can be translated as an

---

[181] Exodus 19ff; 33.

[182] S. Zodhiates, ref. 8334. *Sharath* refers to personal service rendered to an important person. It involves personal devotion and commitment to the one served. (See Joshua 1:1.)

economic and political agenda driven by religious ideals. Hence, the divine promise, *"Every place that the sole of your foot will tread upon I have given you, as I said to Moses"*[183] The "possession of the land" conveys the idea of permanency of residence. The spiritual resource and means by which Joshua would complete his assignment is found in the Book of Joshua, which is pregnant with information:

> *Be strong and of good courage, for to this people you shall divide as an inheritance the land which I swore to their fathers to give them. Only be strong and very courageous, that you may observe to do according to all the law which Moses My servant commanded you; do not turn from it to the right hand or to the left, that you may prosper wherever you go. This Book of the Law shall not depart from your mouth, but you shall meditate in it day and night, that you may observe to do according to all that is written in it. For then you will make your way prosperous, and then you will have good success. Have I not commanded you? Be strong and of good courage; do not be afraid, nor be dismayed, for the Lord your God is with you wherever you go* (Joshua 1:6-9).

Economic Breakthrough: Governed by the Word of God

The successful accomplishment of Joshua's assignment could only be fulfilled by his being totally attached and dedicated to the instructions of the Word of God. In other words, the economic empowerment of the people can only be accomplished spiritually.

---

[183] Joshua 1:3.

This clearly communicates the view that God is completely committed to bringing economic blessings to His people, but He has His own ways of bringing it about. These "ways" are revealed to Joshua when he receives the call and instruction from God. *"Be strong"* (Hebrew *chazaq*[184]) is used to describe *a battle scene*. It conveys the idea of being attached to something, so that one could be obdurate in the face of battle. Joshua's paradigm of God is influenced by his meeting with God as the "commander of the Lord's army." Joshua understood God as a "man of war." By attaching himself to the Word of the Lord, he is assured of victory in the most difficult of situations. Economic breakthrough will come by learning to adhere to the instructions of God's commandments when fighting against the forces of evil that occupy the land of God's people.

Joshua's success or failure is attested to by the extent of his obedience to the Word of the Lord.

Joshua's *attachment* was to the law passed on to him from Moses. "Be careful to *do* (Hebrew *asah*) according to all the law." The word *asah* describes the nature of his employment. It is a word used to describe God's creative ability and the skill involved in fulfilling the objectives. It dealt with refinement. This word is best defined against the backdrop of the Hebrew word *bara* (creation out of nothing). God created everything out of nothing (*bara*) and then fashioned the objects created (*asah*). Joshua's leadership was directly governed and regulated by the law. As long as he remained connected to the law, he would skilfully (*asah*) guidethe people toward possessing their own land and governing it.

---

[184] S. Zodhiates, ref. 2388,.*Chazaq*: to be bound fast, to be attached, to make firm, to be obdurate, to support.

The Law (Hebrew *torah*) was not merely a set of rules or restrictions, but the means by which one could attain the spiritual ideal. In this regard, *torah* could be translated as "teaching," "instructions" and "decisions." The emphasis on Joshua's ministry was on remaining attached to the *word of the Lord since everything he needed to know was to be found in it*. These instructions were passed on by Moses with the intention of guiding Joshua in the difficult challenges that awaited him. Thus, Joshua's whole life was to be saturated in the divine revelation to the point where it spontaneously flowed out of his mouth.[185] He was to "meditate" (*hagah*) upon it both day and night or at all times. He was to muse on it in the light; in the times of rejoicing and sweeping victories. He was to reflect upon it in the dark; in ominous times when the light was twisted away and the darkness rose, heavy and cloying.

Such a lifestyle involves being committed to the disciplines of serious study. *This level of devotion to the Law implied that all the patterns and resources for successful and prosperous living were contained in the Scriptures. His mission would only be successfully accomplished if he obeyed the instructions of the Lord.*

Joshua had to adopt an attitude of fearlessness ("do not tremble [Hebrew *arats*] or be dismayed [Hebrew *chathath*]").[186] His faith had to be in the Law of God. The people of God have absolutely nothing to fear (*arats*). The word *chathath* in its literal rendering means to be broken, abolished, afraid, confounded, alarmed, in fear, in despair, crushed, to terrify and to break. The meaning ranges from a literal breaking to abstract destruction, to demoralisation and finally to panic. It implores Joshua not to crack under

---

[185] Joshua 1:8.
[186] Joshua 1:7.

stress or to be broken into pieces during difficult times. A significant aspect of Joshua's ministry was to have a steadfast *faith in the Word of the Lord.*

Joshua: Living in the Presence of the Lord

Joshua worked closely with the Levitical priest who carried the Ark of the Covenant. The Ark of the Covenant featured greatly in his conquest of the land. He had to follow the Ark carried by the Levitical priesthood. The Ark (*arown* or *aron*) was a container, chest or box covered in gold. It initially carried the Ten Commandments (Tablets of stone), a pot of manna and Aaron's rod that budded.[187] By the time of Solomon, only the Tablets of stone remained.[188] The mercy seat served as its lid. The Ark was the place where Moses met God and received messages from Him.[189] Annually on the Day of Atonement, the high priest would bring the blood of a bull and a goat and sprinkle it on the mercy seat.[190] The "covenant" (Hebrew *beriyth*) refers to a treaty, alliance, pledge and obligation between a monarch and his subjects. In this sense, the ark depicted the place of encounter where God met with His subjects on the basis of the conditions of the covenant. The priests were representatives of the whole nation. This placed upon the people the responsibility of following and submitting to *all* that the ark represents. *Hence, following the presence of God (the Ark of the Covenant and all that it represented) was another important factor in the life of Joshua.*

---

[187] Exodus 25:16; Deuteronomy 10:1-5; Hebrews 9:4.

[188] 1 Kings 8:9.

[189] Exodus 25:22.

[190] Leviticus 16:11-16; Hebrews 9:7.

In the light of all that has been stated, it is evident that God does anoint and empower people to create wealth. Joshua's mandate involved following the divine instruction, fighting great wars by trusting in the promises of God, abiding in the presence and thereby eliminating the hostile kingdoms in Canaan so that the Israelites could receive their inheritances. The Scriptures clearly state that man does not have the power to create wealth; this is the sovereign act of God:

> *Then you say in your heart, "My power and the might of my hand have gained me this wealth." And you shall remember the Lord your God, for it is He who gives you power to get wealth, that He may establish His covenant which He swore to your fathers, as it is this day* (Deuteronomy 8:17-18).

However, prosperity is not an end in itself; it is the means to bring a blessing to the nations. It is not motivated by selfish desire but by the will to add quality to the lives of people in the earth. In being blessed, God desires His people to be a blessing. This includes addressing the disparities and imbalances in the Church globally. The Church is the design of God to establish, instruct, teach and guide His people in the way that they should conduct their whole lives. It is through divine guidance that people can enjoy qualitative living and navigate their course through life's challenges. The Church is also the medium through which God has purposed to release His sovereign will into the earth. The absence of the true Church will cause decay and darkness in the earth. The Church is the salt of the earth and the light of the world. If the world is in decay, then the Church has lost her "saltiness"; if the world is in darkness, then the Church has lost her light. God is deeply involved in the process of economic reformation. By empowering godly people (just like Joseph and Joshua) in the world of economics (and in other facets of society), He seeks to bless humanity as a whole. The Church plays an integral role in being the *resource centre* that provides the information for business enterprises.

Regrettably, there were noticeable shortcomings in the ministry of Joshua. However, the Church can learn even from these. He did not totally conquer the land.[191] Yes, he was successful in bringing the nation into fruitfulness and inheritance; however, the people were then divided according to their tribal allotments, thereby focussing on their personal breakthroughs. At the end of his life, the tribes were fragmented according to their allotted inheritances. They became materialistic and sought personal gain. It is notable that in the entire Book of Joshua there is no reference to any attempt by Joshua to build God a house or establish Him a kingdom. In addition, Joshua did not leave a successor and he did not develop a team to pursue and complete the task ahead of him. His death left the people without a leader and without direction.

Programme of Conquest

The Israelites clearly missed the main reason for their empowerment. The programme of conquest was not merely a resettlement programme implemented by God so that He could honour His promise to the patriarchs of old. There was a divine motive that transcended the quest for rule through territorial acquisition.

In the initial implementation of the programme of conquest, the Israelites adopted an attitude of intolerance toward the alien nations they were invading. They violently eliminated all forms

---

[191] Read Joshua 13:1-15; 16:10.

of life established by these nations, burning cities and destroying idols and other cultural practices of these peoples. As harsh and cruel as this may be, they were following divine instructions. Wherever they conquered, they were instructed to establish a new order of life with new religious practices that were distinctly different from those of the alien nations. These directives were a crucial part of a divine plan to restore a way of life and governance in the earth that was in accordance with the Kingdom of heaven. God does not permit a displacement of any people unless He has a good reason for it.

According to Moses, God does permit a removal of those systems of life that encourage *wickedness* in the earth.

> *Do not think in your heart, after the Lord your God has cast them out before you, saying, "Because of my righteousness the Lord has brought me in to possess this land"; but it is **because of the wickedness of these nations that the Lord is driving them out from before you*** [my emphasis] (Deuteronomy 9:4).

The divine motive for wanting to bless and prosper His people is the desire to use these people as a means to indict and displace lawlessness and fraudulent practices in the earth. Anything that does not encourage godliness must be removed. Only that which sustains life and brings back wholesome living is what releases the favour of God into the human arena. God handed over the rule of the land to the Israelites because of the wickedness of the nations who occupied it before them. He desires for His people to bring back godliness and righteous living in the earth. Hence, whenever the nation of Israel practised disobedience and turned from the laws of God, they too experienced the wrath and judgment of God.

This is probably the reason for the very turbulent history of the Israelites. Holistic living can only be accomplished by living according to the laws and commandments of the Creator. He has the recipe for life, since He has created all things. God will not be a pawn in world systems that have been tailored by deficient humans. He sets the rules for wholesome living and we must follow accordingly.

When we pray, we take the initiative to invite God back into His rightful place in our lives. God is being petitioned to restore His order in our lives, thus removing evil in the earth. We cry to God for His wisdom to pervade our wisdom and for His will to be done in the earth. God must become the axis and foundation to everything we do. Therefore, prayer is the posture that dynamically reflects total dedication to God. We invite Him to possess everything we have and invade our lives with a kingdom that will bring righteousness, peace and joy in the Holy Ghost. We give Him the freedom to speak and influence our lives. We tell Him that His counsel is the only source that can rebuild and redeem the inhabitants of the earth. Our prayer also precipitates the cry for forgiveness of our wicked ways.

> *If My people who are called by My name will humble*
> *themselves, and pray and seek My face, and turn from*
> *their wicked ways, then I will hear from heaven, and*
> *will forgive their sin and heal their land*
> (2 Chronicles 7:14).

Apostolic Reformation and Economics

In this present season, God is releasing an anointing on the Church to create wealth. If the believers and Church leaders follow the patterns set out in the Scriptures, they will receive the assurance of great breakthroughs in personal lives, businesses and in the Church at large. When the Church is assembled, every aspect of Kingdom lifestyle and business must be discussed. This includes economic matters. People must be trained to be successful in the marketplace. However, congregations must model this in the culture of their gatherings. The congregation must be a visible reflection and example of how the Kingdom of God functions in the earth.

The spirit of poverty must be ruthlessly destroyed in the mindsets of the people. Poverty is not the state of one's bank account but the state of one's mindset. God's desire is that people enjoy prosperous living, although He warns against covetousness and wealth being a goal in itself. Godly gain must produce contentment. In the majority of the world,[192] poverty is a serious problem within and outside of the Church. However, I am convinced that if people are correctly instructed, they will break through this bondage and experience the blessings of God. Poverty is a direct result of the fall, as is sickness and so many other scourges in the world. The Apostolic Reformation is calling for the *re-formation* of all things back to their original state in the earth. There must be a conquest of this spiritual and physical state of being.

Congregations must re-evaluate their paradigms about finance and their understanding of why economic empowerment of the people is so important. In the Apostolic Reformation a very clear economic policy must be set that goes beyond the traditional concepts of money matters. Economics affect every sphere of life. We, the Church of Jesus Christ, are about to inherit the largest piece of real estate—the planet Earth. Preparation for this must precede the actual conquest. The Church must prepare their Josephs, Daniels, and Zerubbabbels to rule the earth. The key financial principles in

---

[192] Previously referred to as third world or disadvantaged communities.

the Word of God must be extracted and then installed into the lives of believers so that they can be successful in life.

Apostolic congregations must become the first fruit of economic breakthrough in every region in the earth. Such congregations must prove to the sceptics and to the unbelievers that the economic policies recorded in the Scriptures do work. They must test it in the laboratory of their own "houses." They must demonstrate faith in God's Word, in adverse and hostile circumstances, that clearly proves that the cruse of oil will not run out until the need is met and that a boy's lunch can feed a multitude.

In this regard, Church leaders must be encouraged to critically analyse and re-evaluate the view adopted with regards to the Church's approach to their own method of running the treasuries of the congregation. There must be a movement away from a need-centred "bless me" mentality to an enterprising one of empowerment and financial independence. *If the treasury of the congregation (head) is not run according to biblical principles, then naturally there will be a malfunction of the body (believers) in the area of finance.* The anointing flows from the head downwards. This is the pattern set out for us in the Psalms.[193] If the financial systems of congregations are not built on the theocratic model, they are set to fail. Compliance with the Word of God (as we learn from Joshua) is a fundamental prerequisite to financial breakthrough. For example, if the corporate structure does not tithe, how can they expect the believers to do so?

Tithing in the Apostolic Reformation

Congregations must transition from the law of tithing to the spirit of tithing by being an example in this respect. If churches

---

[193] Psalm 133.

want to eat the corn of the field in the first year of their transition, then they must follow the principles learned at Gilgal.

I am of the opinion that the treasury of a local congregation must tithe of its whole income received. This is a divine principle. If it is followed, it will provide supernatural blessings naturally and become the genesis of a continuous lifestyle of giving. By tithing, the Lord is acknowledged as the source and provider of all income. The Scriptures are emphatic: *The tithe is the Lord's.*[194] According to Malachi, it provides protection and insurance against the devourer.[195] The tithe principle is the school master instructing and nurturing a lifestyle of giving. This will include all those who are employed by the Church or receive a salary from their congregations. Every income earner must be a tither.

According to the principle of tithing, the tithe must go to the storehouse. In essence, the storehouse in the Old Testament was not the magnificent Temple but the priest who worked in the Temple. According to the Old Testament, the tithe was used to pay them salaries, to ensure that they lived comfortable lives. There is no record of the tithe being used primarily for the building of the Temple. This was done from special offerings taken.

In the New Testament, the personnel who labour among the people are the storehouse. When people bring their tithes, it is to primarily sustain and provide for those who supply spiritual sustenance among them. From this we glean a principle that the tithe must be given to the storehouse. In the context of local congregations, the tithe must go to the storehouse(s) of that congregation. This begs the question to be asked: Who is our storehouse(s)? Who are the ministries that

---

[194] Leviticus 27:30.

[195] Malachi 3:10-11.

give us care, sustenance and provision? The storehouse is not mission organisations, charities, airfares for travelling into mission fields and so forth. Just as those ministering in the local congregation must be taken care of by the tithe of the income of the local congregation, so must those who minister into the congregation be remunerated. The storehouse could be a network, a denomination, an Apostle or a ministry that they submit to and from which they receive spiritual instruction, resource and support. If the principle is adhered to, there will be a release of unprecedented blessings upon every ministry.

Is any member of the Body of Christ exempt from this principle? I am of the opinion that this is not so. It is applicable to everyone in the Church—from the poorest to the richest. Can anyone not afford to honour this principle? Absolutely not, since the tithe is the first fruit of all income...by this I mean that the first thing that must be done when income is received is to take out the tithe before any other payment is made. Strictly, the tithe is the only thing that everyone *can* afford to pay. Local treasuries must pay the tithe first and then everything else. Could it be that it is in this area that many congregations have robbed themselves of untold blessings?

The second payment should be toward the salaries of their staff and not the mortgage and other expenses. Only after the salaries are paid should other expenses be met. If the storehouse is lacking, then a curse is released upon the entire congregation. If there are insufficient funds after following the principles of tithing to meet all the other needs of the house, then the congregations must trust God for the miracle of multiplication to take place. The miracle lies in trusting and faithfully following the instructions of the Lord. The Lord will not fail in keeping His promises.

If you test the principles, you will discover that the Lord is faithful to His Word.

The Church must move to a lifestyle of giving beyond the tithe. There can be no harvest without sowing. This involves the process of faithfully giving of one's tithes and offerings. Every believer must understand the unprecedented potential locked up within him or her when he or she develops the culture of giving. *Believers must seek to give so that they may give more.*

In the Apostolic Reformation, congregations are called to transition from the mentality of "bread for the eater" to that of "seed for the sower." Apostolic communities are motivated to give more than to receive. It is an integral part of the "sending principle." They seek to invest in Kingdom projects rather than personal projects. Personal interests and selfish desires are superseded so that the agenda of God may receive precedence. The culture of giving is birthed in one's poverty and not in the abundance of one's riches. The diverse needs of the giver will always oppose the desire to give liberally. However, it will be prudent to observe this truth: *One may be able to count the number of seed in an apple, but only God can count the number of apples in each seed.* It is more blessed to give than to receive.

If we are to reclaim that which is lost, we must exercise spiritual expediency in a hostile environment. Presently there is a great shift taking place in the Church of Jesus Christ. The Holy Spirit is releasing an anointing that endows people to overcome and successfully exercise ministry in the marketplace. Unusual opportunities are befalling Christian business people. However, fundamental to success is the necessity for total devotion and commitment to the Lord. These believers are required to obey the Word of the Lord and be totally desirous to propagate the divine purpose rather than their personal dreams. These individuals must choose to live in the presence of the living God at all times.

The present Reformation of the Church requires that a clearly defined biblical policy is developed and taught to the people. In a world of abject poverty and great distress, the Word of God does have the solutions to the problems of the world. God wants to raise the Joseph anointing in the Church. The primary objective of the Apostolic Reformation is to mobilise and empower people to a place that is beyond self-sufficiency. It is to make them prosperous and extremely resourceful, thereby facilitating the process of building His Tabernacle and establishing His Kingdom. It is only through God's way that the world will experience endless peace and prosperity.

Recapitulation

We have discovered through the pages of this book that the Church is on a pilgrimage governed by the directives released in the heavens. The purposes of God are unravelling into the earth through the medium of changing seasons. These are known as *kairos* moments, allowing for the confluence of spiritual things to unwrap themselves into the Church and demand that adjustments and change be implemented. The climaxing of these divine moments induces levels of crises, thereby provoking a response. At these precise moments leaders must act decisively. They need to also surround themselves with wise counsel. Gilgal is the place that provides insightful advice. It is a signpost directing the Church to keep on the pathway of truth. More than that, Gilgal is an encampment where leaders must stop over in preparation for the next phase in the journey. The following points summarise the principles extrapolated from Gilgal for churches to negotiate the transition into the Apostolic Reformation.

First, the people must be mentally prepared for the next stage in their journey. Mental reconfiguration is accomplished by learning how to use the prophetic anointing to prepare their mindsets for the way forward. The prophetic anointing removes erroneous concepts and ideas (old foundations) that will hinder the journey forward. It gives sight to the blind and illumination to darkened minds. If leaders do not reconstruct the mindsets of the people, then the people will find themselves in the valley of inactivity and rebellion to the purposes of God.

Second, leaders must establish the apostolic principle(s) into the foundation of that which they are required to build. This involves the process of building by following the divine pattern. The Bible contains all the details for building accurately. By associating with legitimate apostolic ministry, they engage the spirit of the "wise master builder" that is present to supervise the building programme. Remember that Apostles and apostolic congregations build *people* and not structures, edifices or dogma. If people are built by engaging divine wisdom, then Christ will be standing in the earth through these "pillars."

Third, we learn that there cannot be any movement forward in any new season without going through the painful process of circumcision. Only the circumcised are credentialed to be an integral part of God's household and have the right to herald the good news in the earth. The circumcised are the "born again" community of believers who model to the earth in an exemplary way the spirit of true community. They are the "epistles" of God written and read by the world.

Fourth, the Cross of Christ becomes the centre of everything that is done. The efforts and labours of the Church are merely the result of the grace of God. Without the meritorious work of Christ, nothing can please God. The Passover teaches the Church that the victory is already completed and that the Church can minister from a place of rest.

Finally, new seasons bring to the Church new opportunities. Gilgal teaches us that God wants us to eat of the produce of the land. The programme of conquest empowers the Church to take back its rightful place in the world. For the Church to come to that governmental position, it must review the way it manages finances, since biblical correctness in this area is fundamental to coming into a literal possession of the land.

Bibliography

Barrett, C.K. *The Signs of an Apostle.* The Cato Lecture 1969, Paternoster Press, London, 1970.

Conner, Kevin J. *The Church in the New Testament.* 2nd Edition. Conner Publications, Blackburn, Victoria, Australia, 1987.———. *Interpreting the Book of Revelation.* Acacia Press, Victoria, Australia, 1995.

Ruthven, Jon. *On the Cessation of the Charismata, The Protestant Polemic on Postbiblical Miracles.* Sheffield Academic Press, Sheffield, Australia, 1993.Sparks, T. Austin. *Prophetic Ministry. A Classic Study on the Nature of a Prophet.* Destiny Image Publishers, Shippensburg, PA, USA, 2000.

Tenney, Merril C. *The Zondervan Pictorial Encyclopedia of the Bible.* Vol.2 D-G. The Zondervan Corporation, Grand Rapids, Michigan, 1975, 1976.Van Gemeren, Willem A. *Interpreting the Prophetic Word. An Introduction to the Prophetic Literature of the Old Testament.* Zondervan, Grand Rapids, Michigan, 1990.Zodhiates, Spiros. Managing Editor, Warren Baker, D.R.E. *The Hebrew Greek Key Study Bible,.* Revised Edition. New American Standard Bible, AMG Publishers, Chattanooga, 37422, USA, 1991.

THE HISTORY OF THE SOUTH AFRICAN
APOSTOLIC MOVEMENT (1980-2008)

APOSTOLICITY

THAMO NAIDOO

APOSTOLICITY: The History of the South African Apostolic Movement (1980-2008)

Within South African Pentecostal circles has emerged a movement of variegated streams, named in this study as the Apostolic Movement (AM). Proponents of this movement call for a return to the 'apostolicity of the church.' The AM draws attention to the nature, hierarchical structure and mission of the church, introducing 'new' and contrasting perspectives to those traditionally held by Pentecostal churches.

This study focuses on the history of Apostolicity in the AM streams that have emerged and developed through three periods: the 1980s, 1990s and 2000s. While there are several other streams in the AM, this study has a specific focus on the following South African AM groups: New Covenant Ministries International (NCMI), Grace International (GI), Congress World Breakthrough Network (C-WBN), International Strategic Alliance of Apostolic Churches (ISAAC) and Judah Kingdom Alliance (JKA).

Connect with the author:
www.thamonaidoo.com

Twitter: @thamonaidoo
Facebook: https://www.facebook.com/thamo.naidoo
Instagram: @thamonaidoo

Apostolic Gate
Instagram: @apostolicgate

Gate Ministries Sandton
Twitter: @gatesandton
Facebook: facebook.com/gate-ministries-sandton
Instagram: @gatesandton

eGenCo

Generation Culture Transformation
Specializing in publishing for generation culture change

Visit us Online at:
www.egen.co

Write to: eGenCo
824 Tallow Hill Road
Chambersburg, PA 17202, USA
Phone: 717-461-3436
Email: info@egen.co

f facebook.com/egenbooks
youtube.com/egenpub
egen.co/blog
pinterest.com/eGenDMP
twitter.com/eGenDMP
instagram.com/egenco_dmp

32147102R00086

Made in the USA
Middletown, DE
24 May 2016